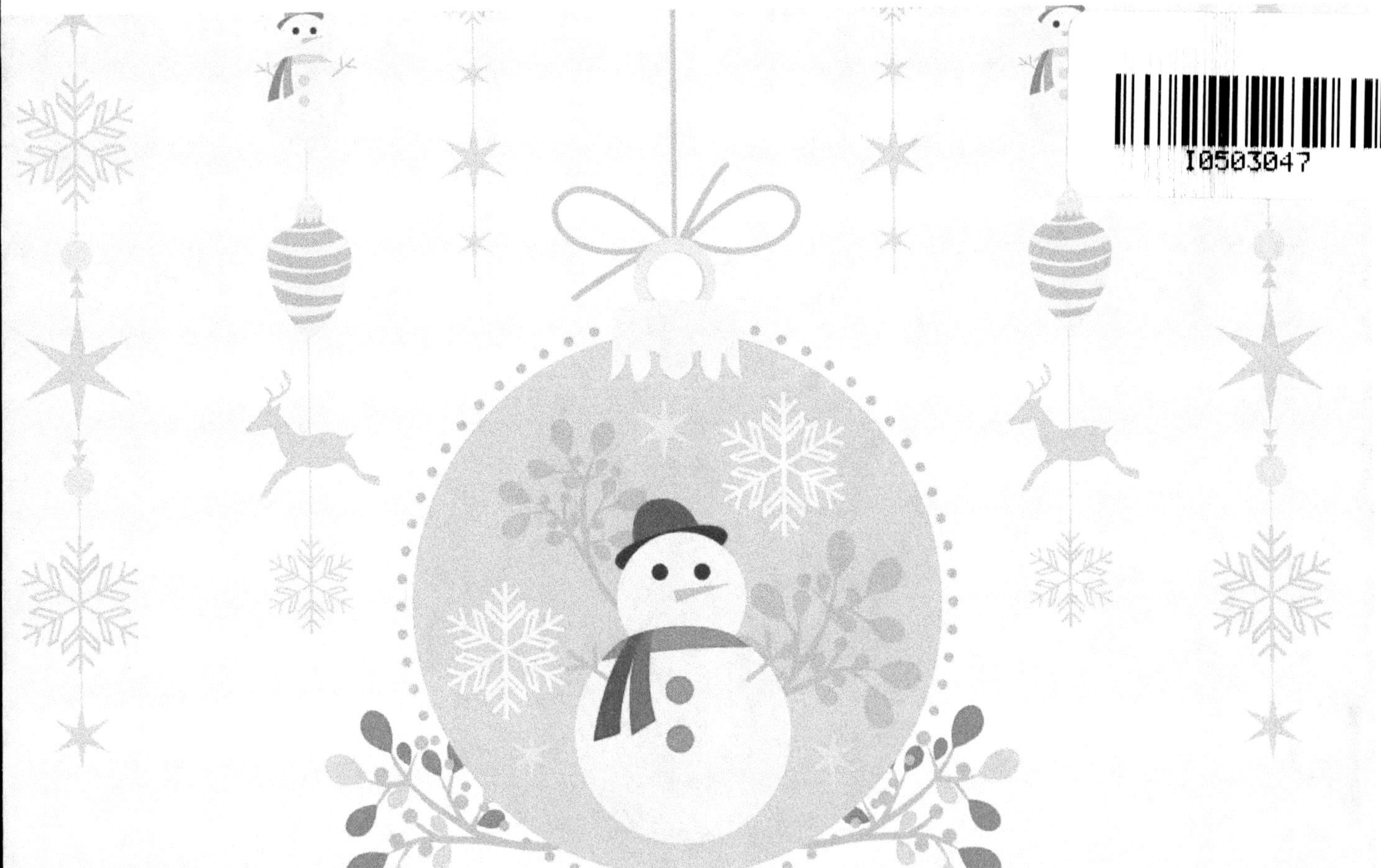

Merry
CHRISTMAS

This Books Belongs To

....

....

....

....

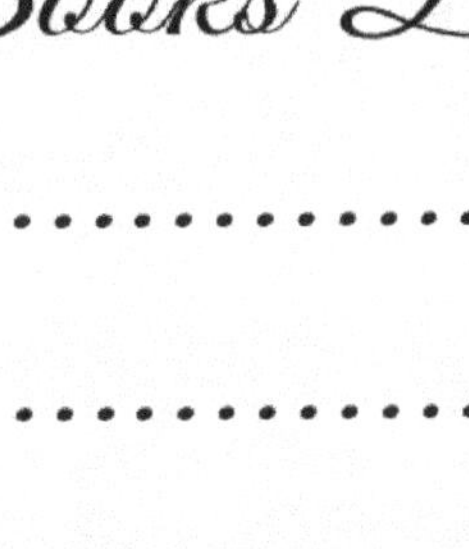

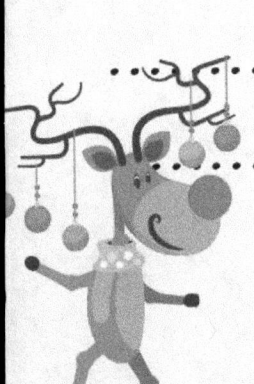

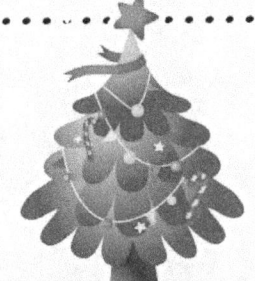

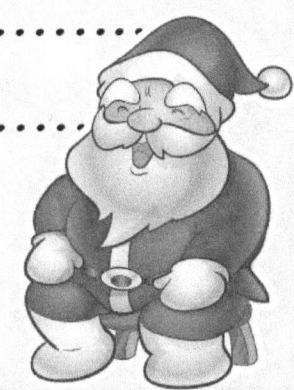

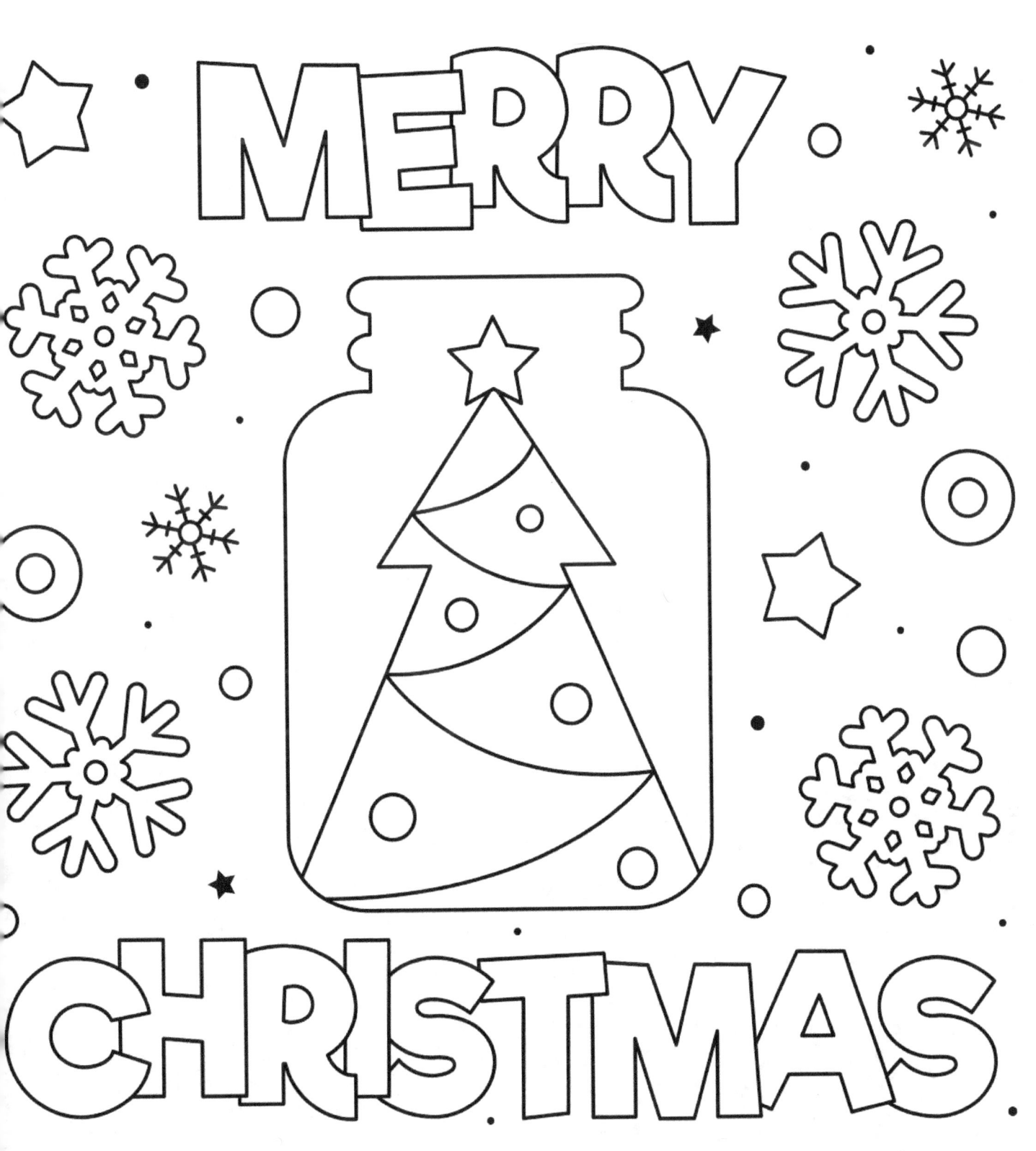

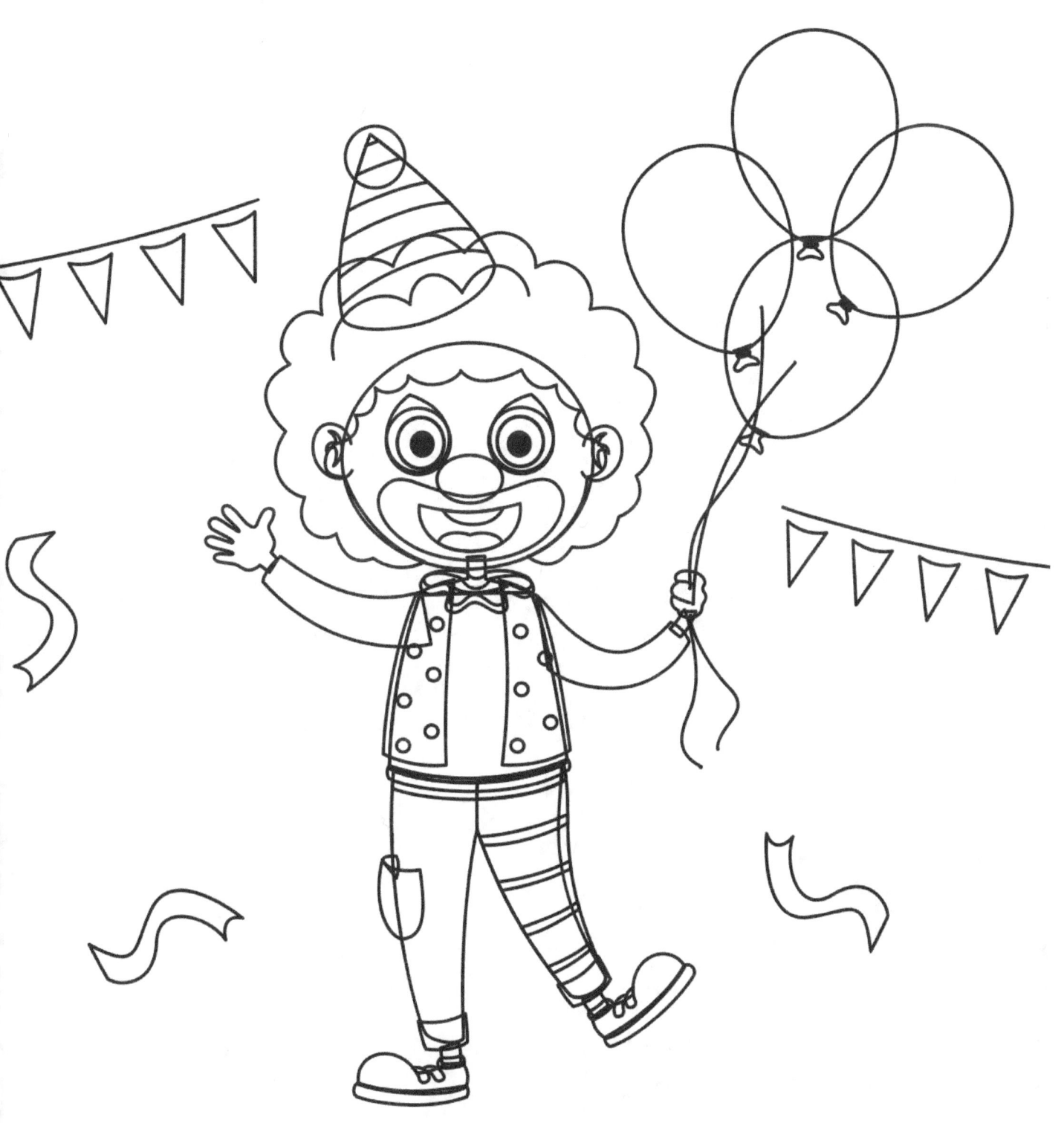

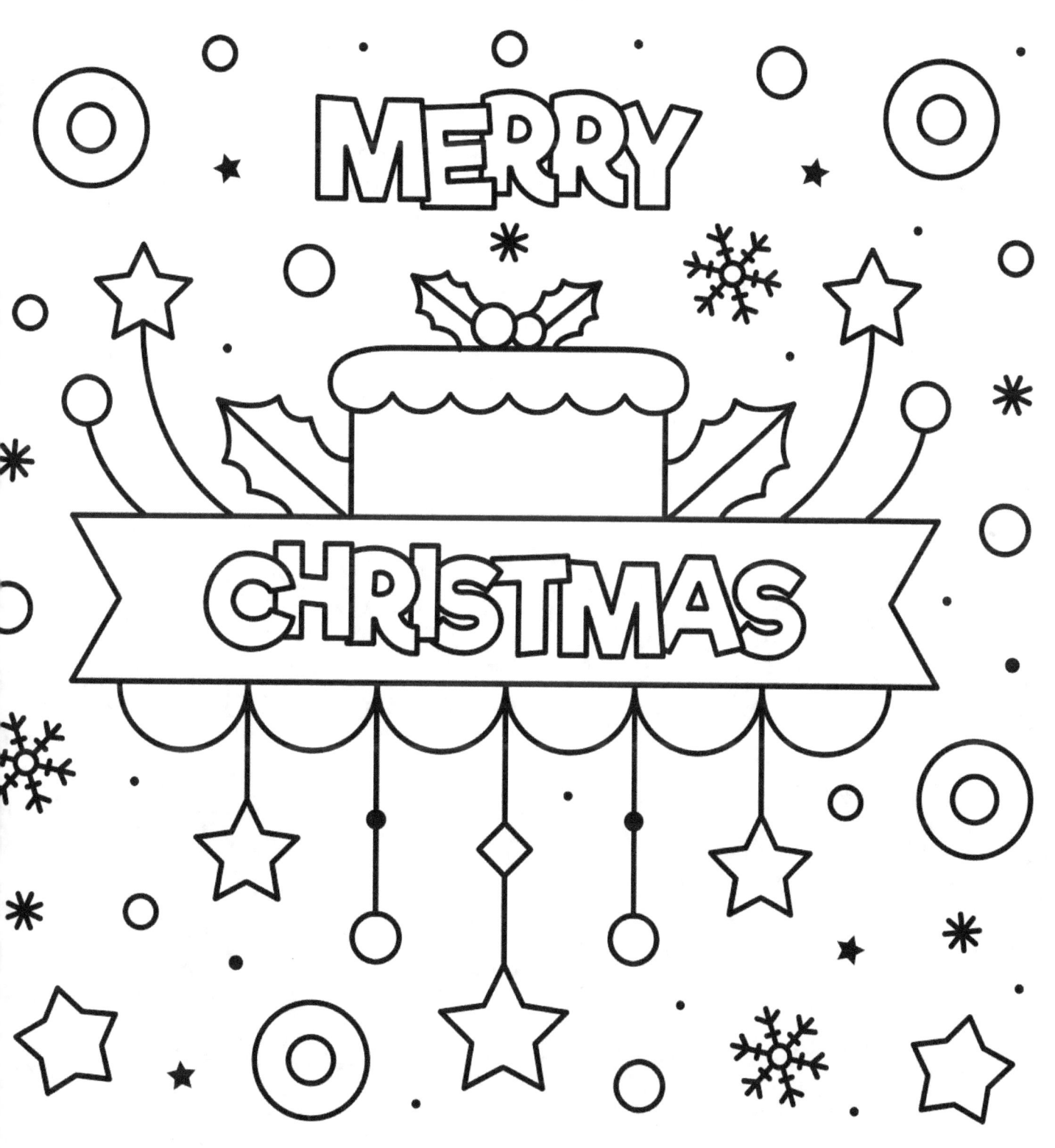

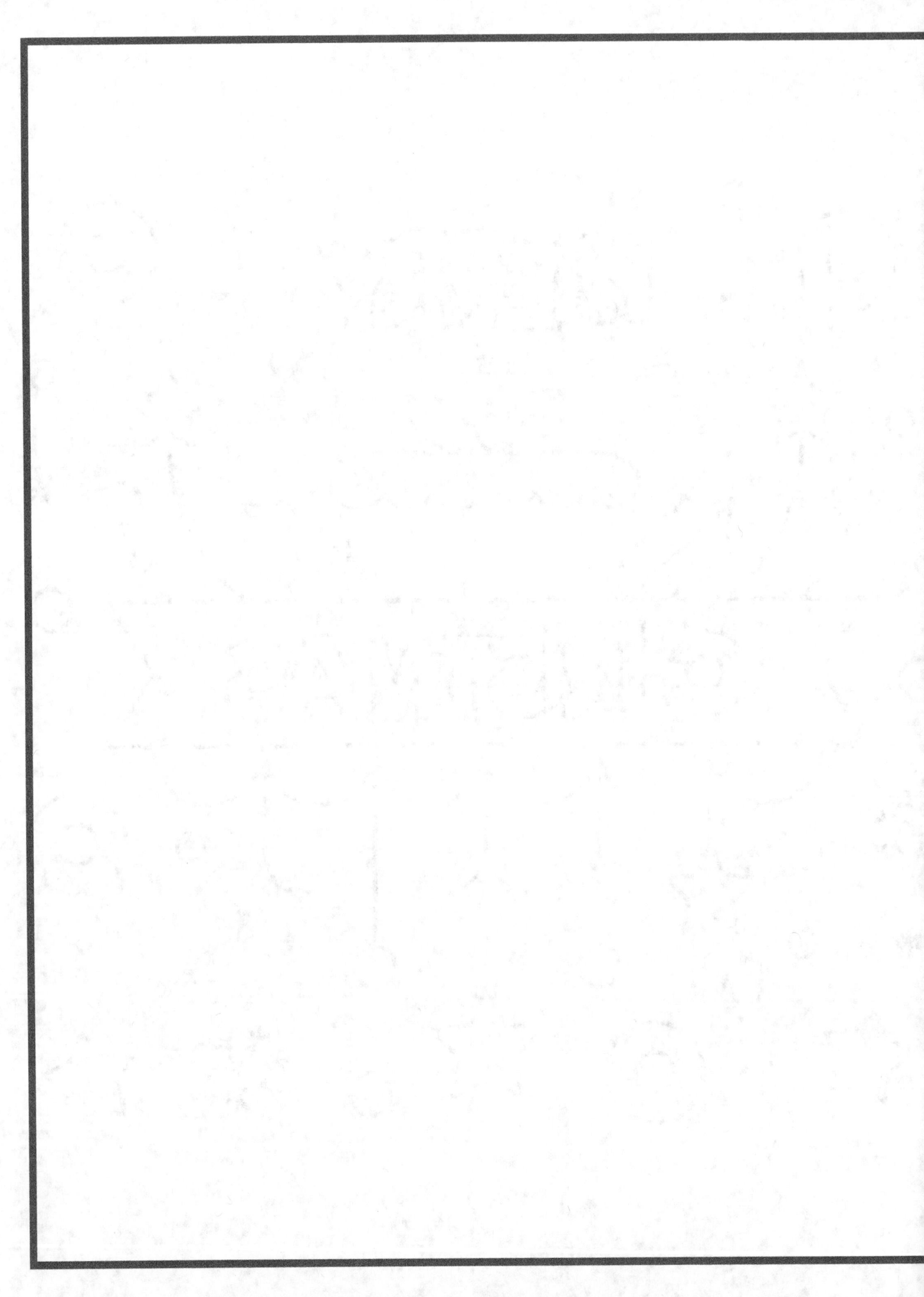

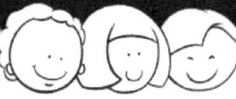 

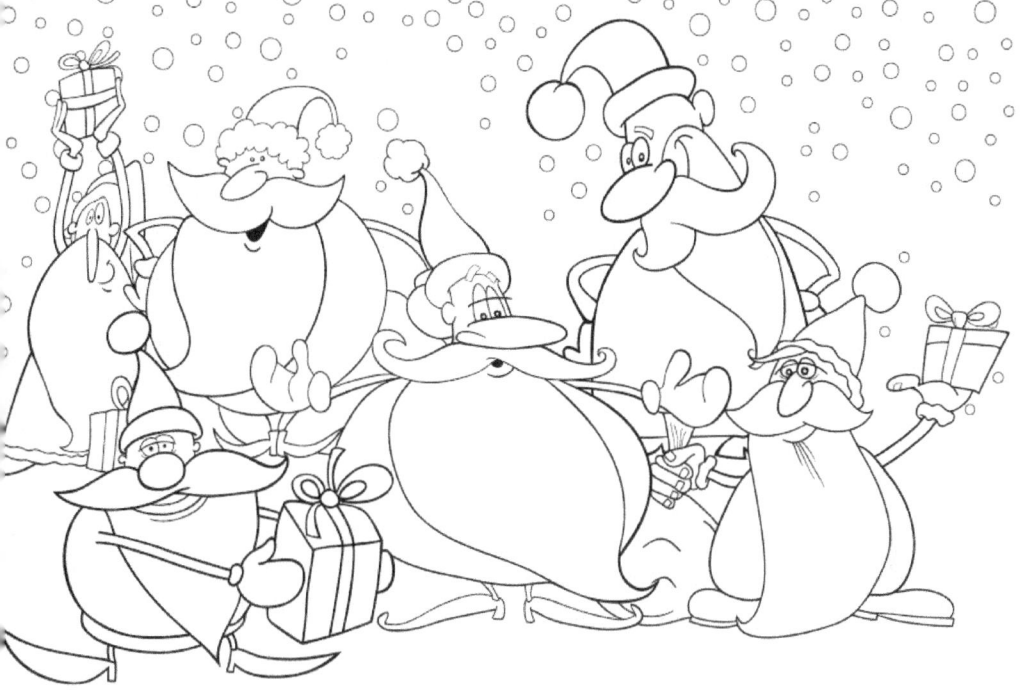

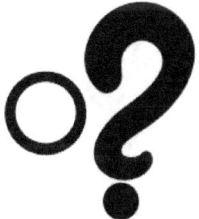

FIND
7
DIFFERENCES

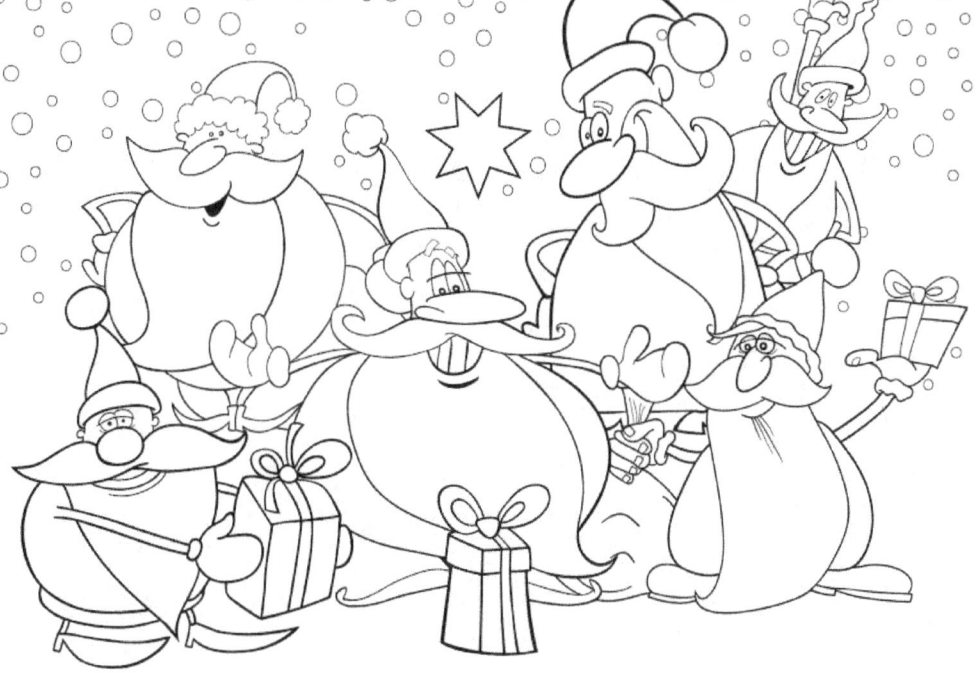

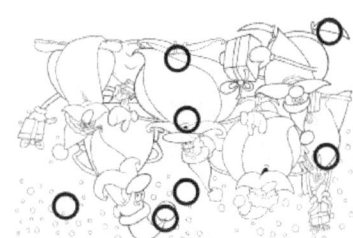

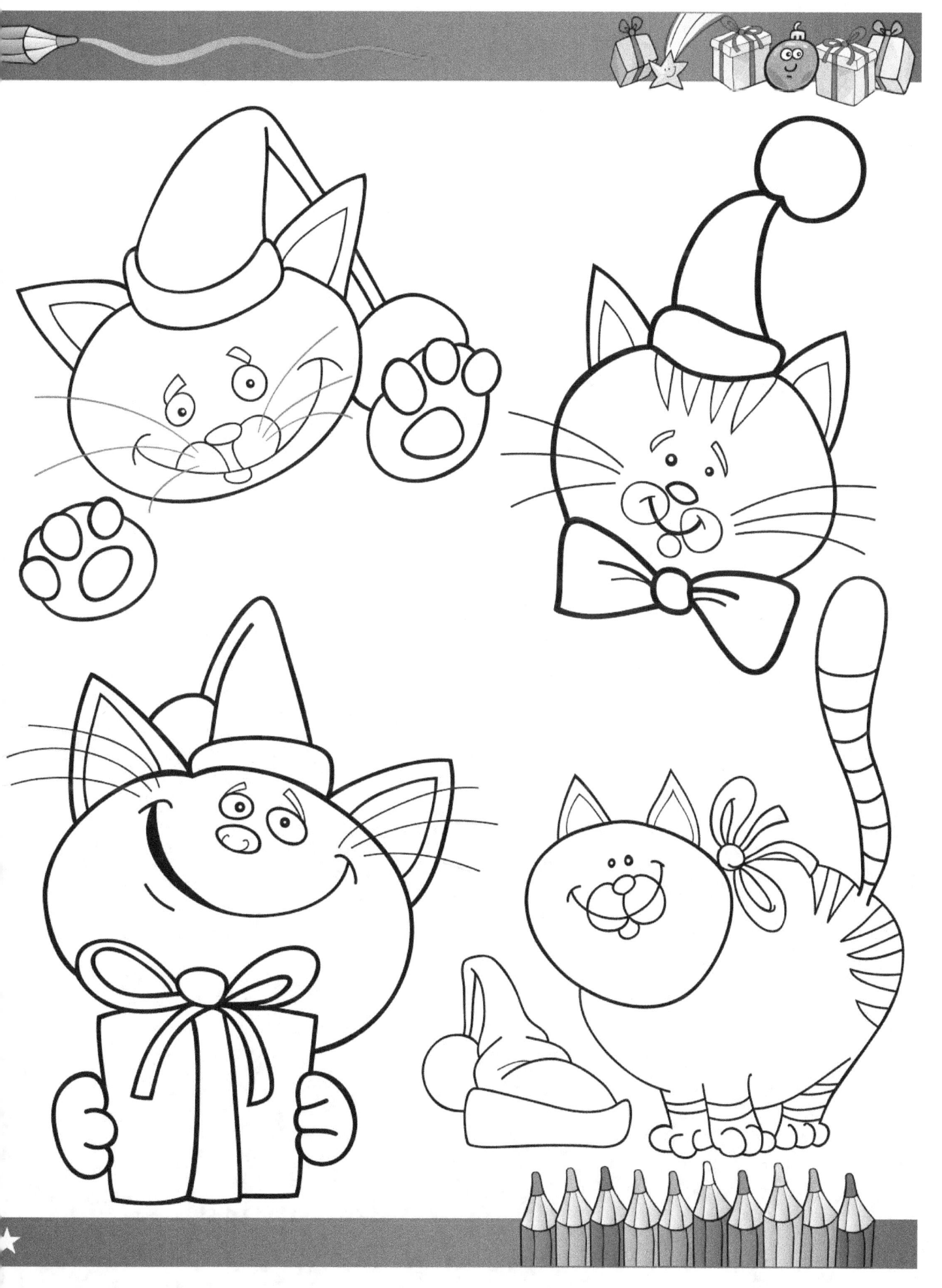

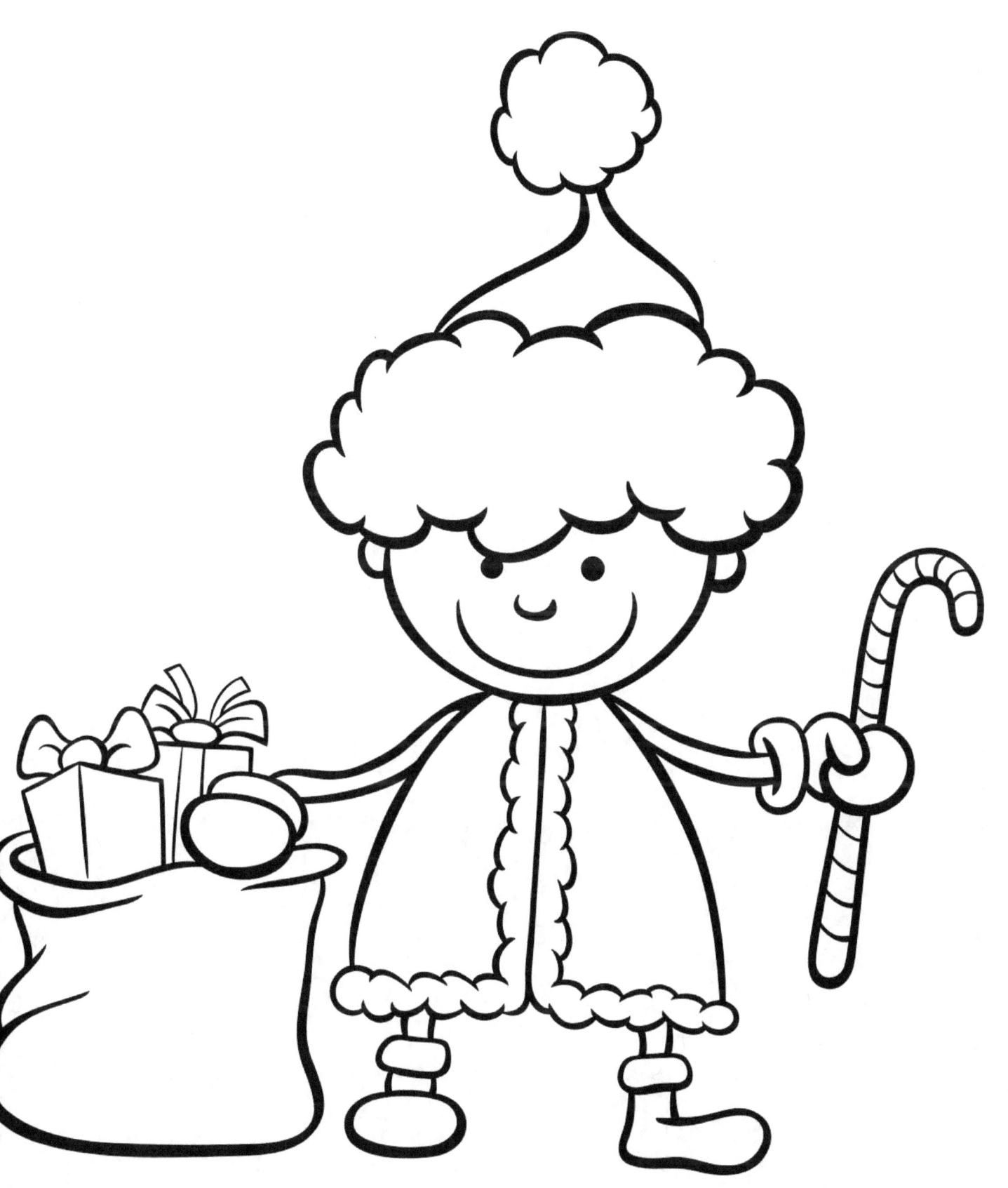

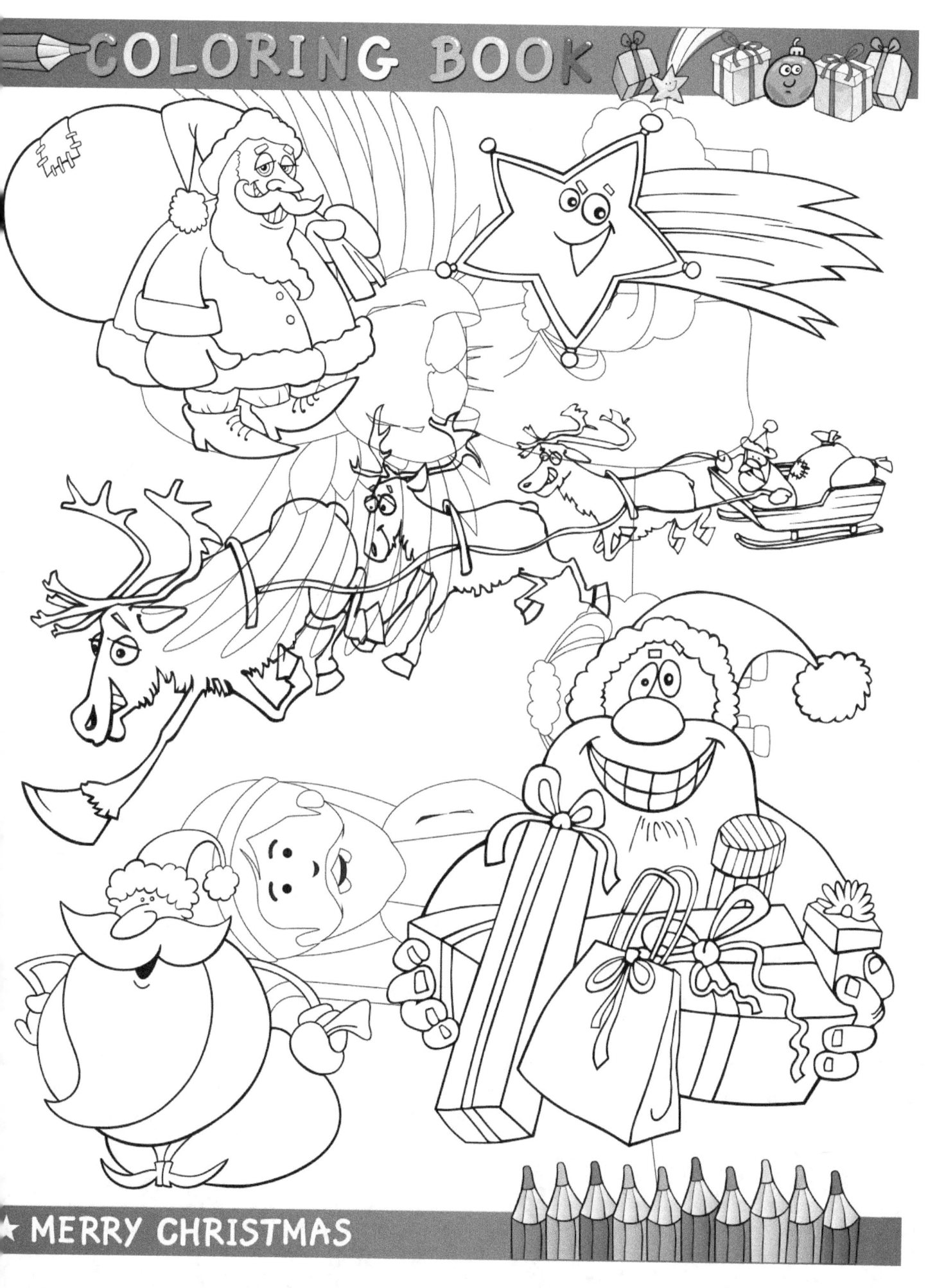

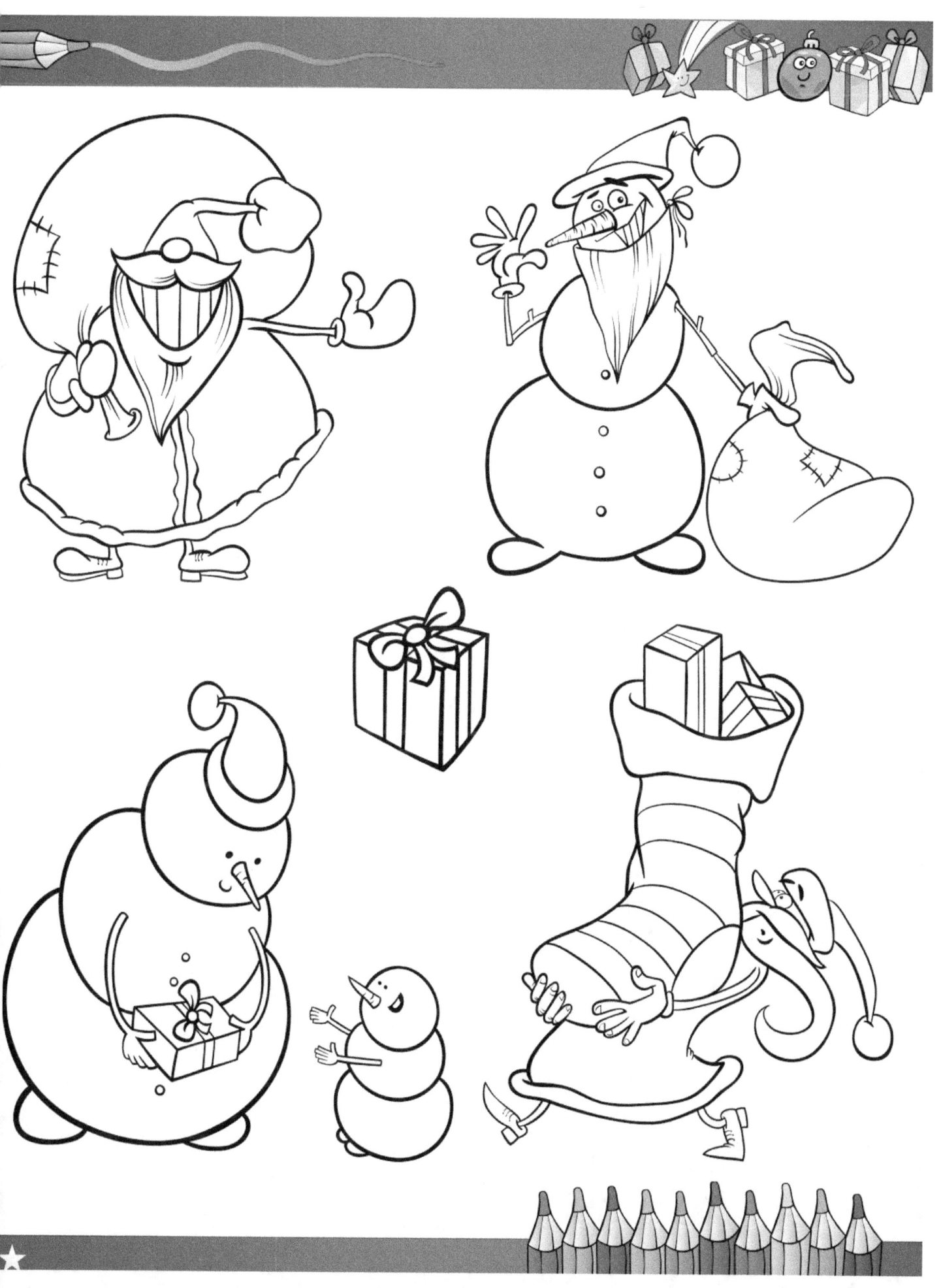

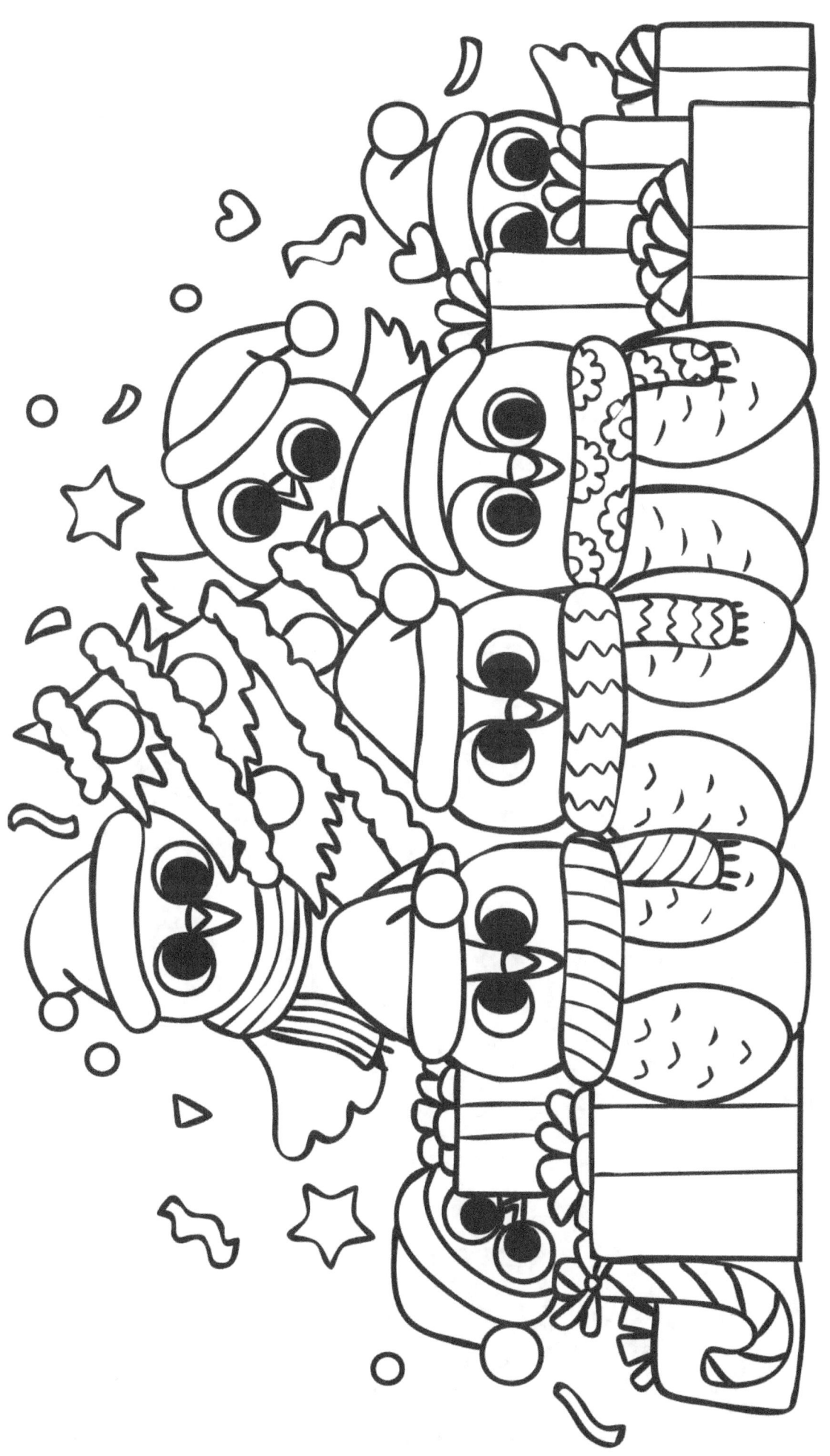

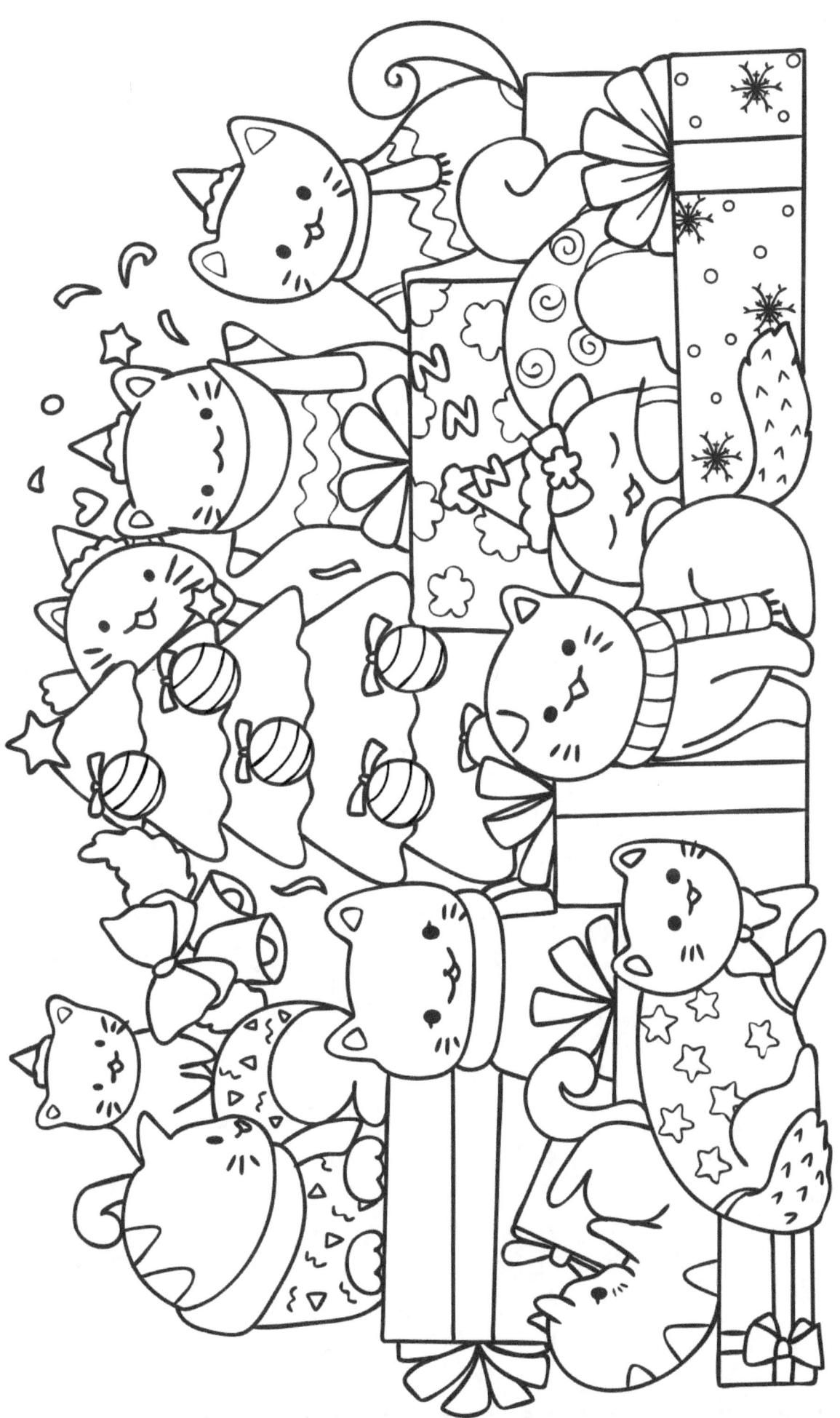

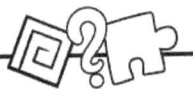

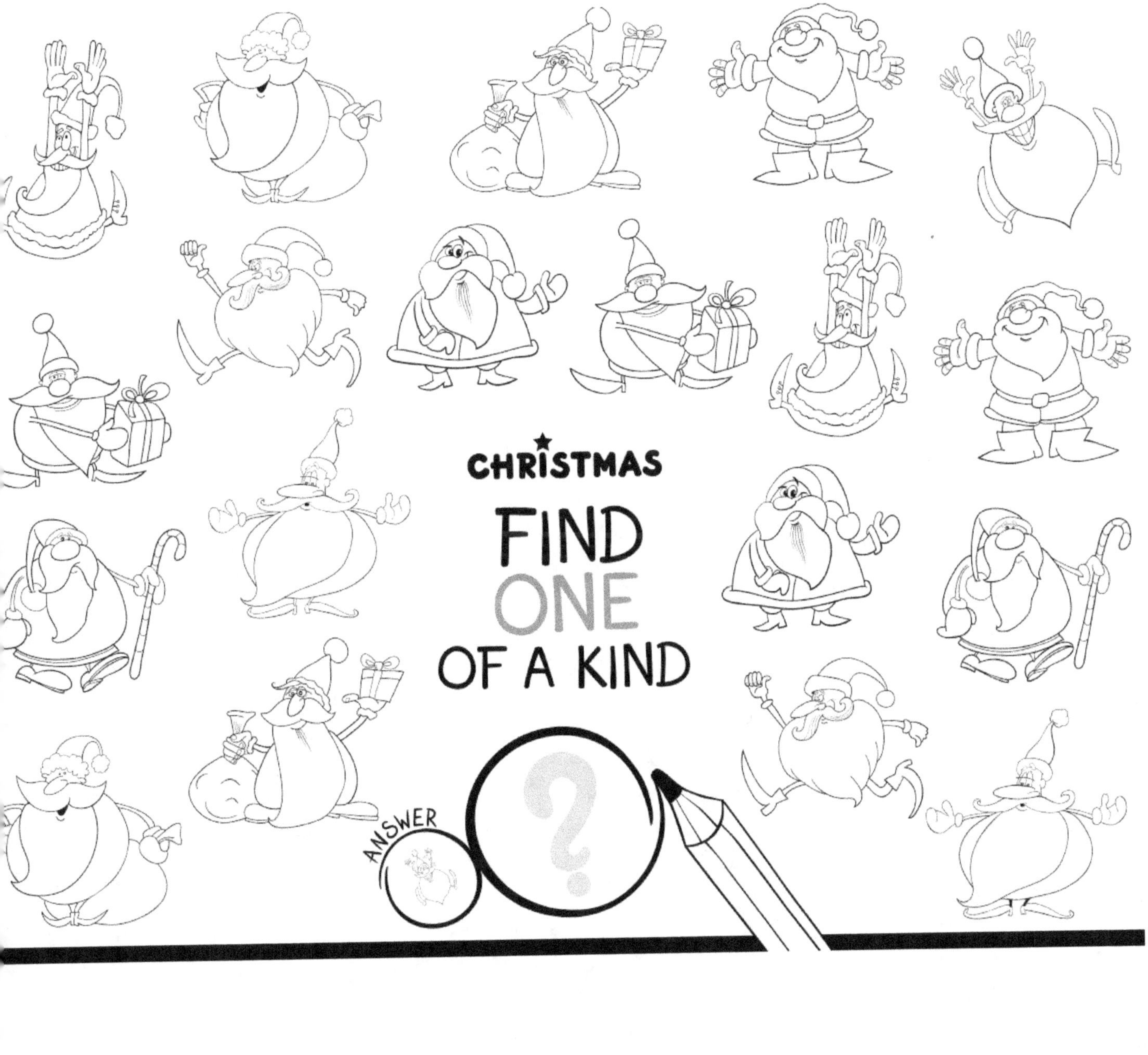

CHRISTMAS

FIND
ONE
OF A KIND

ANSWER

?

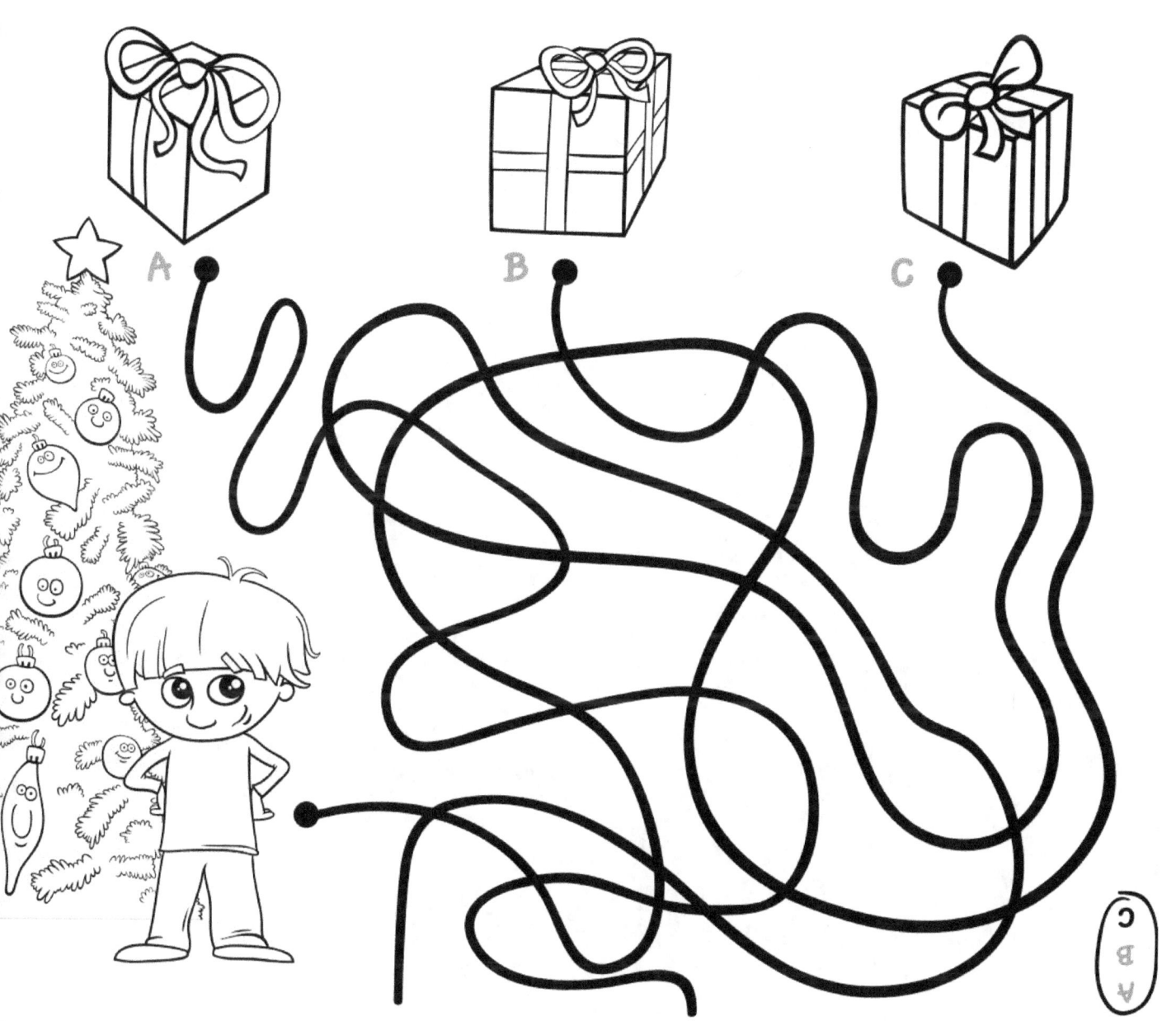

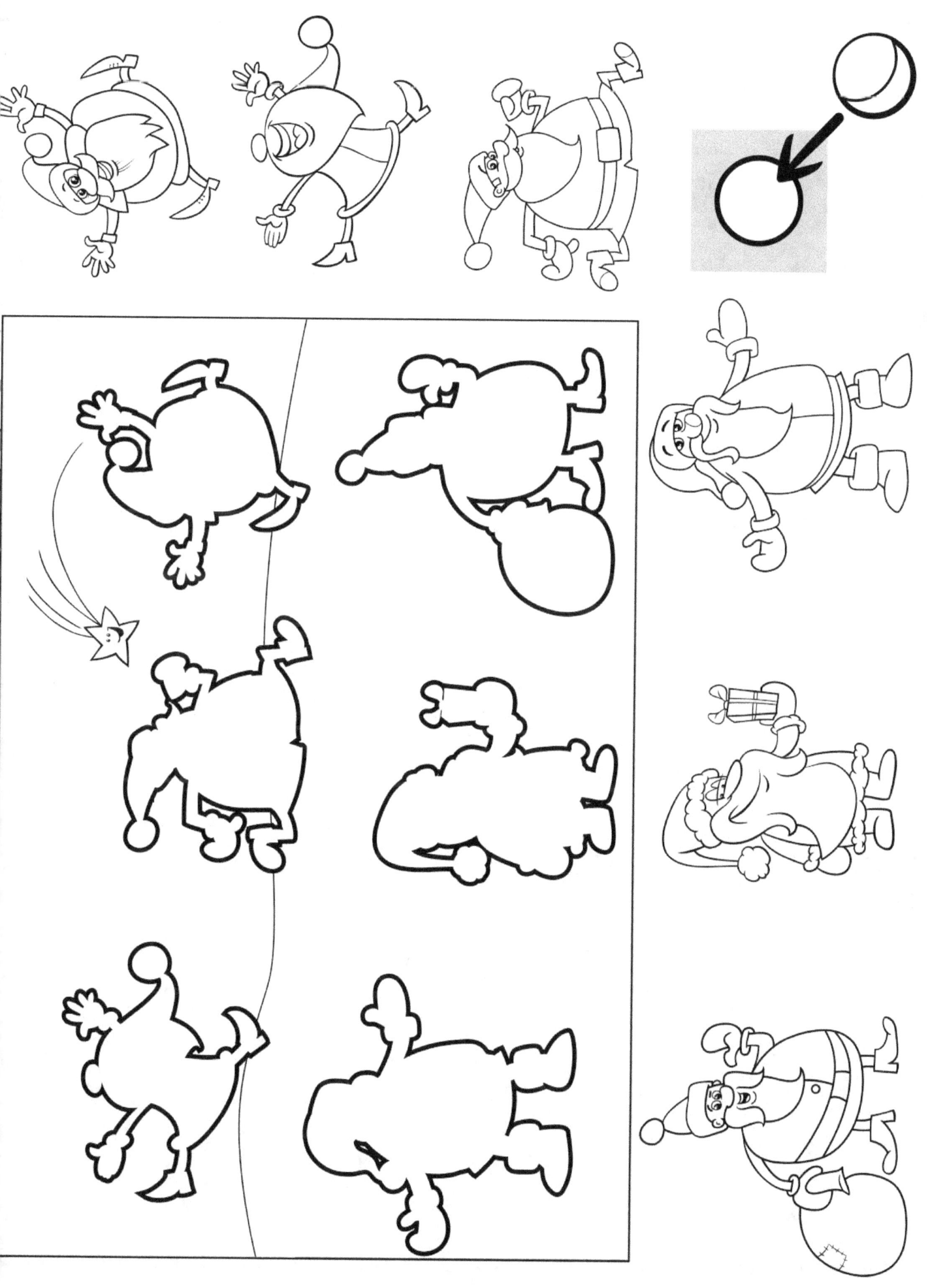

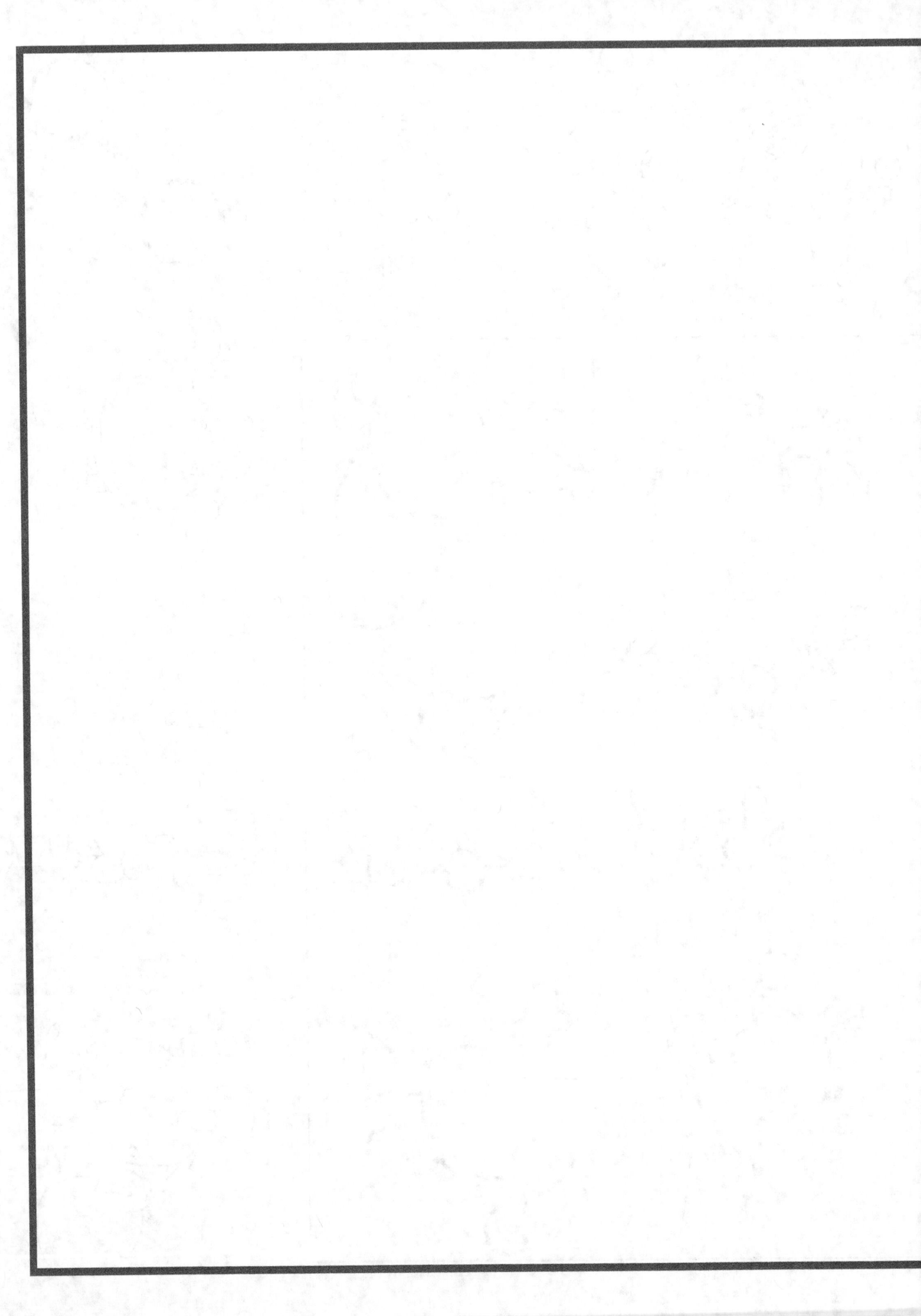

WHAT COMES NEXT?

1

2

3

4

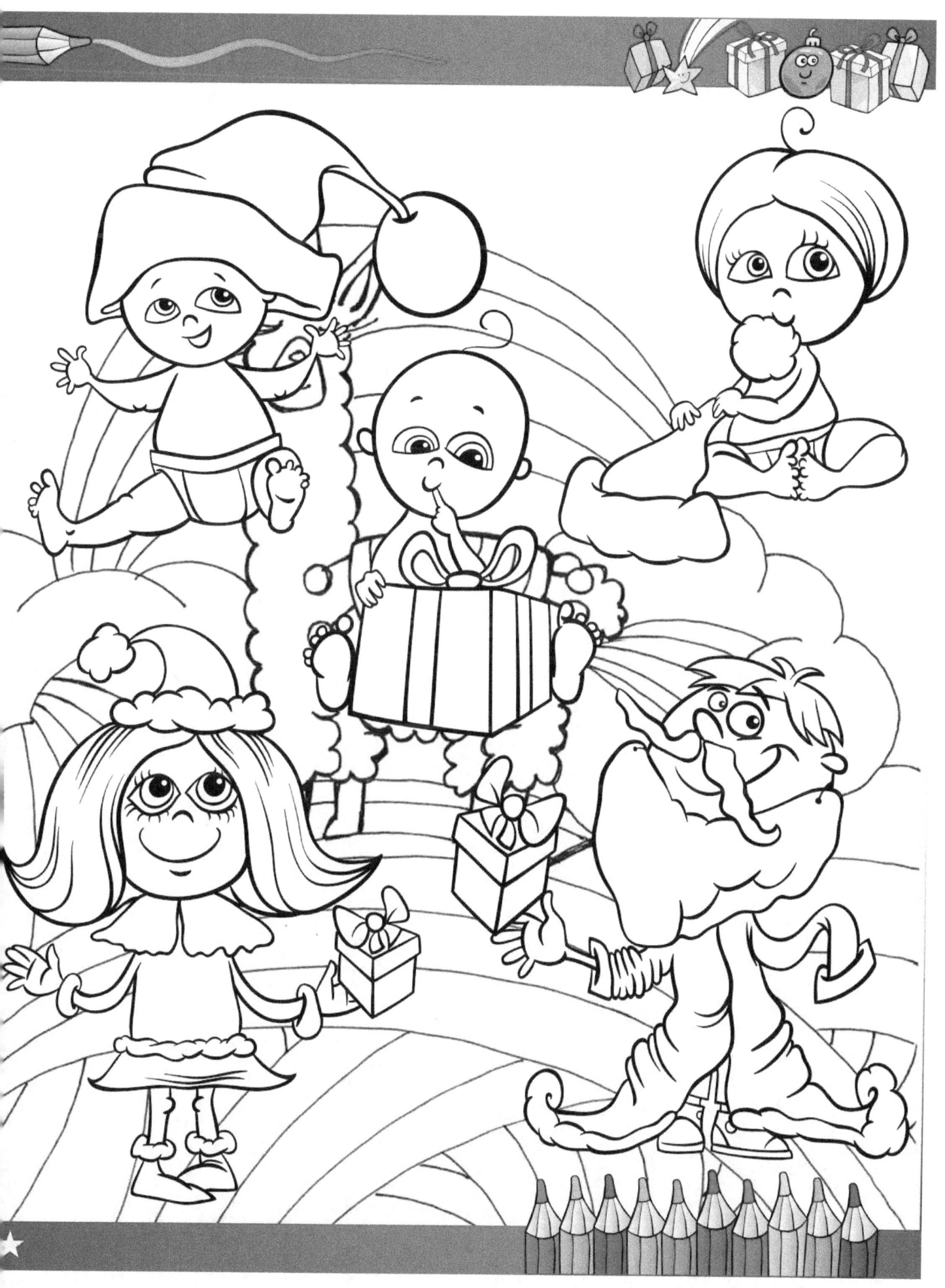

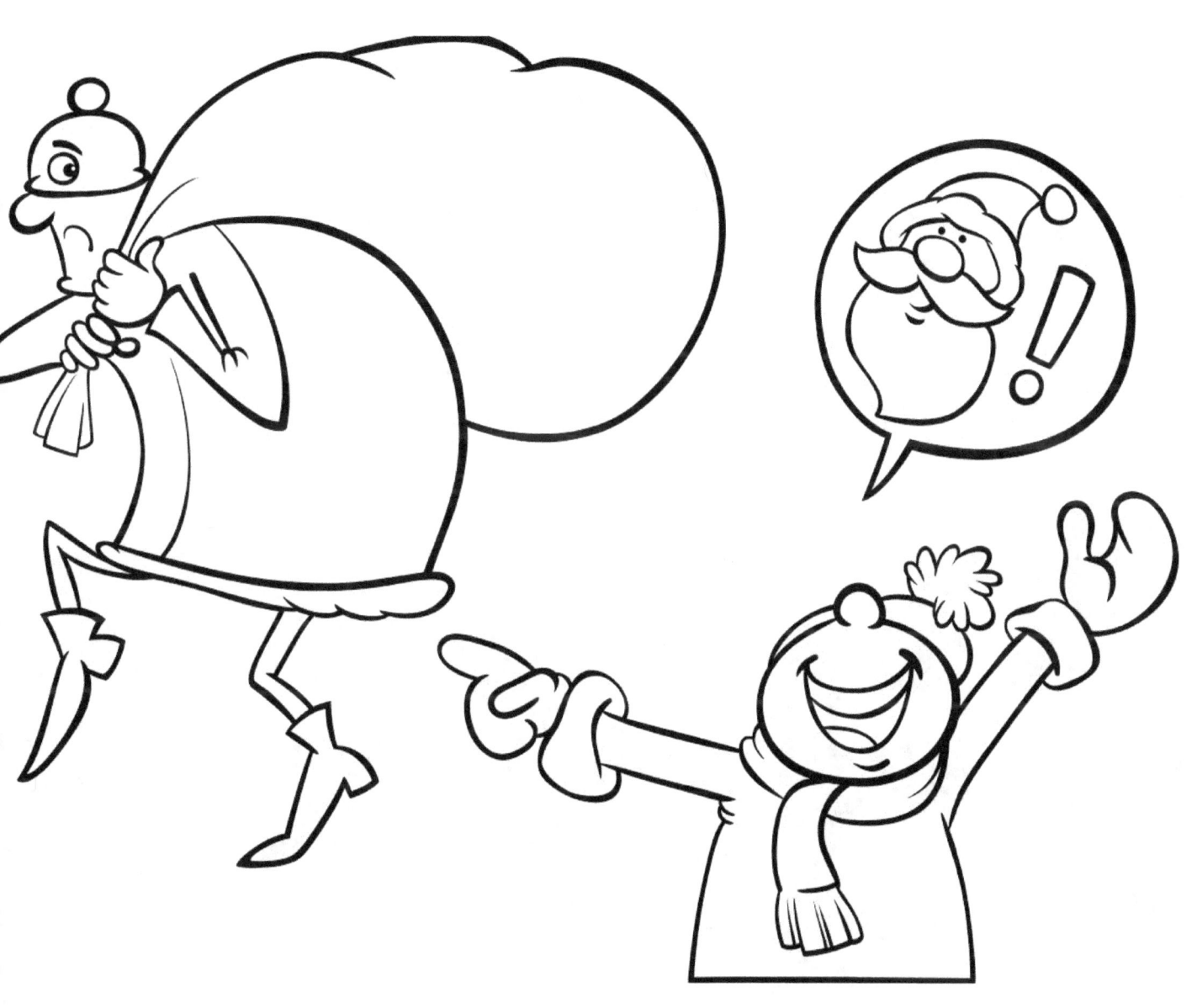

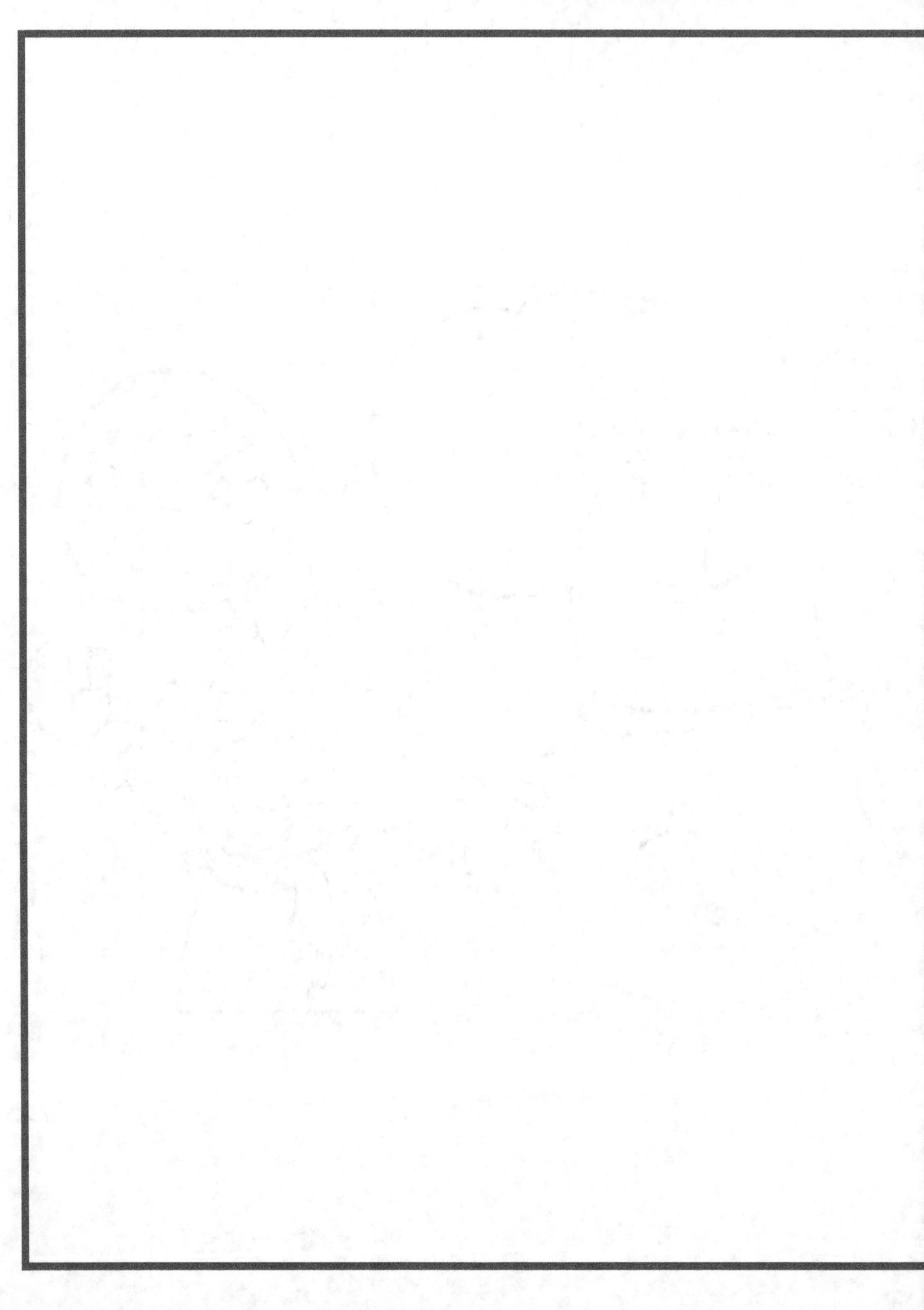

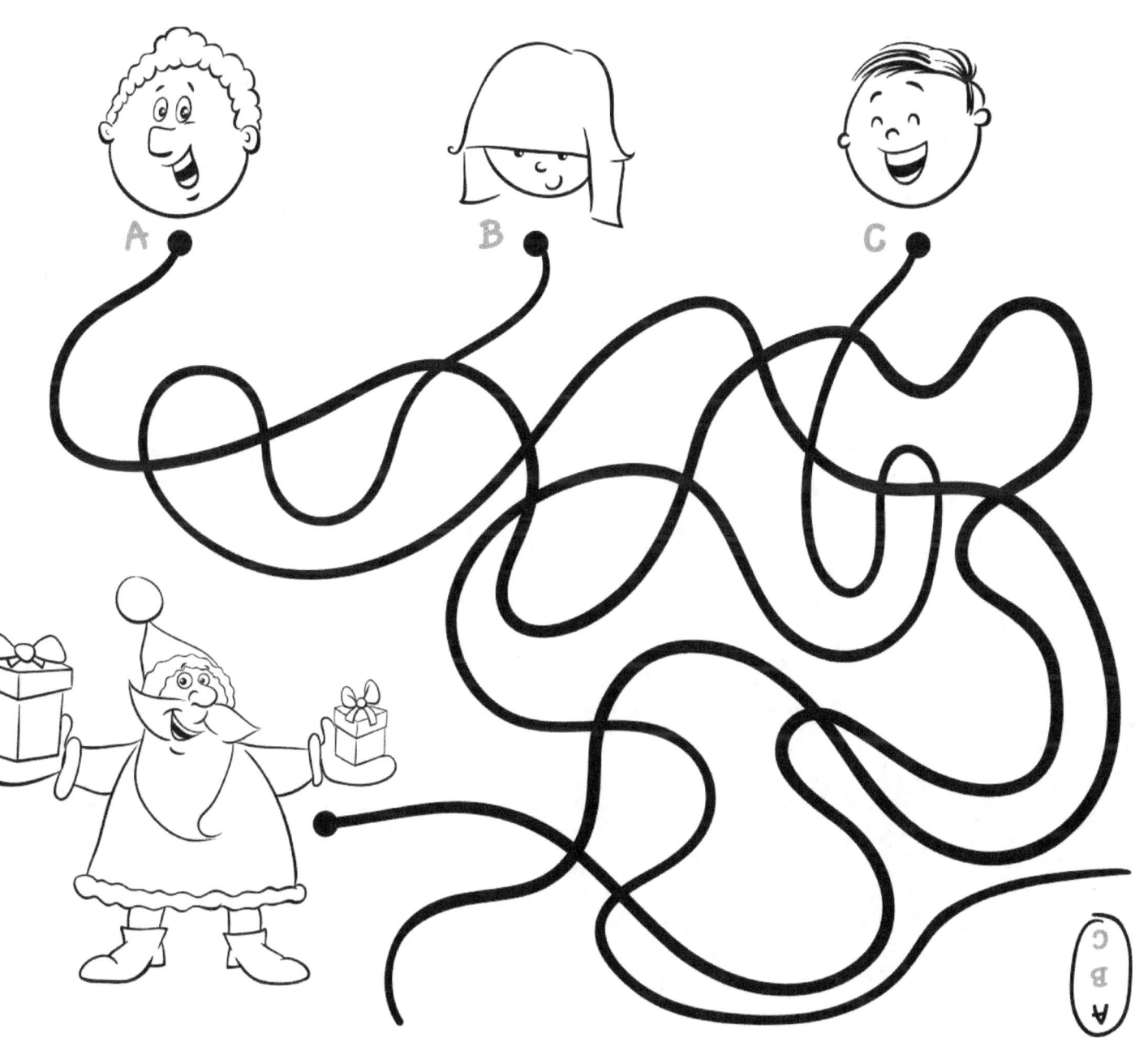

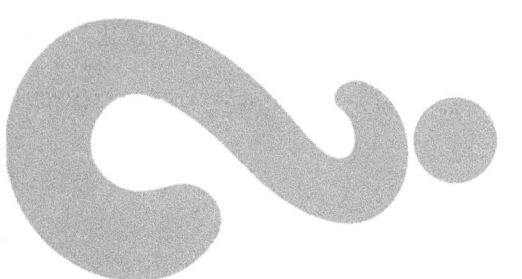 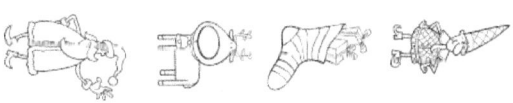

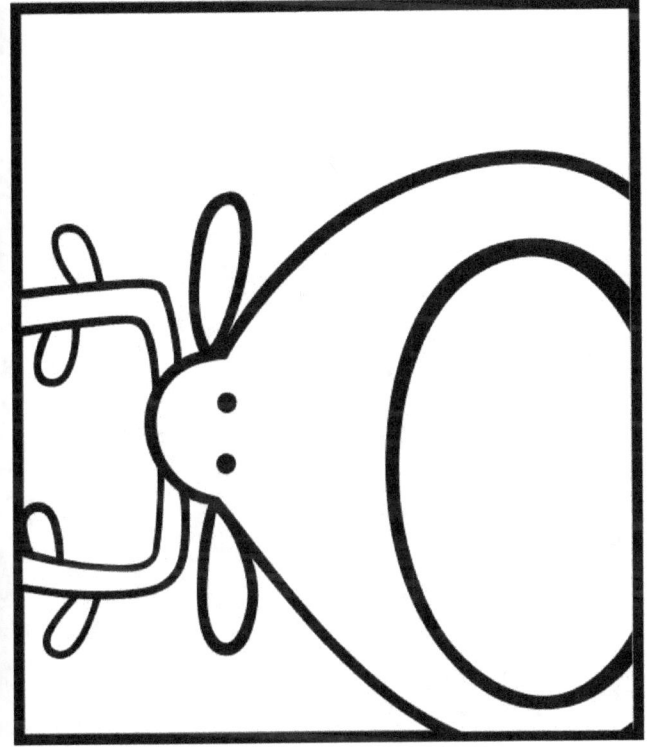 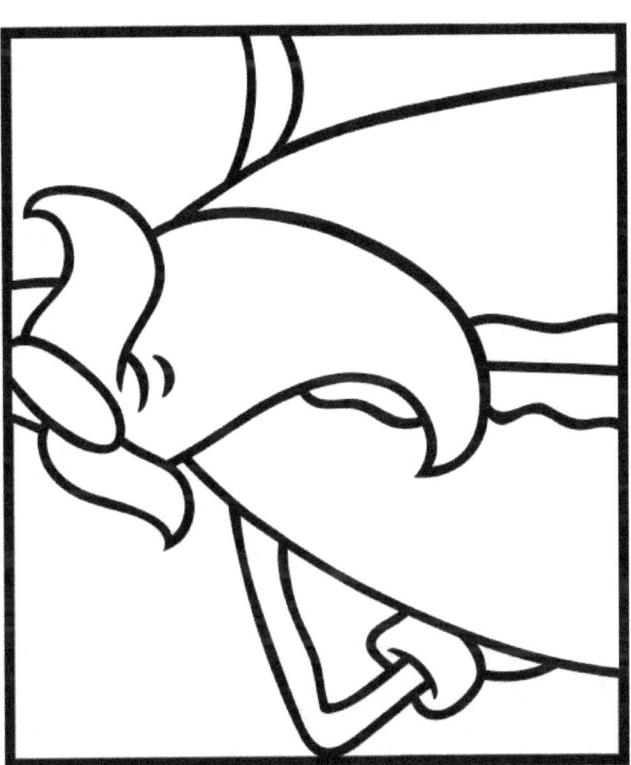

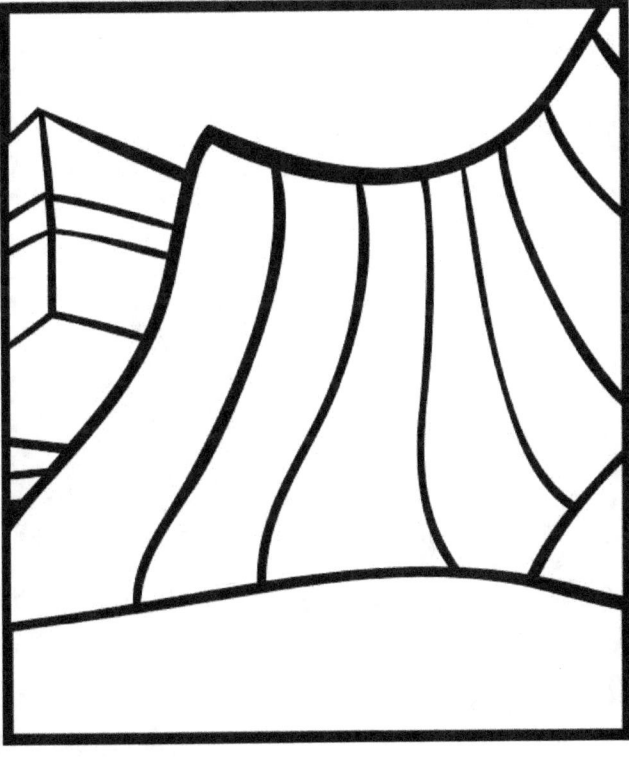 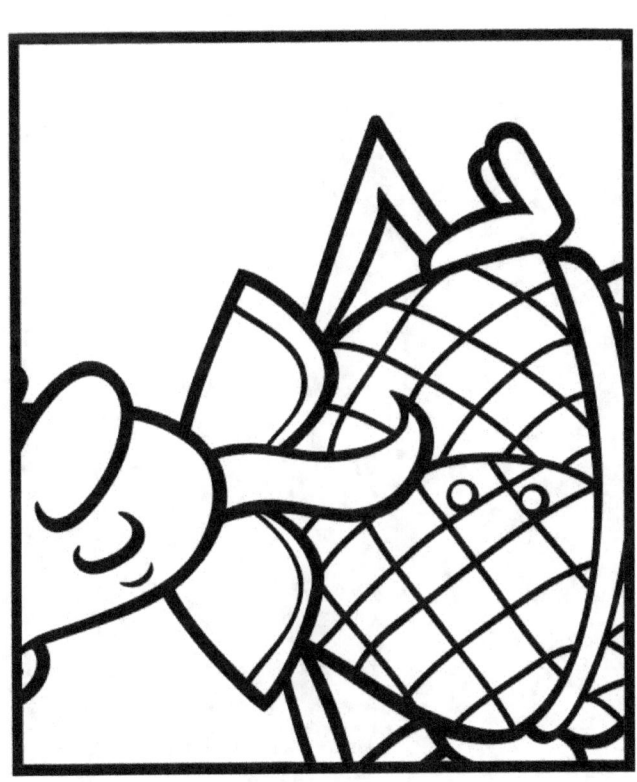

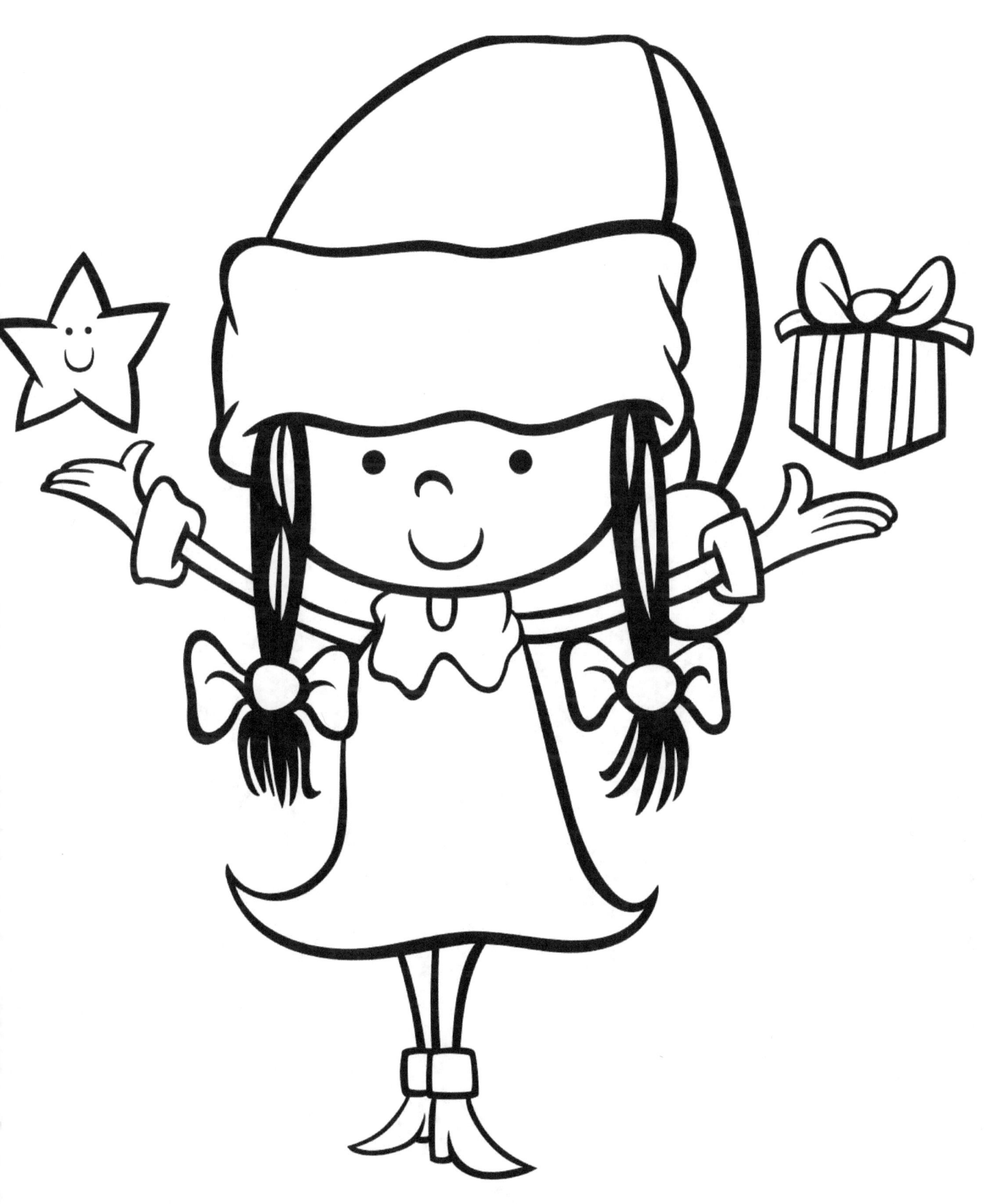

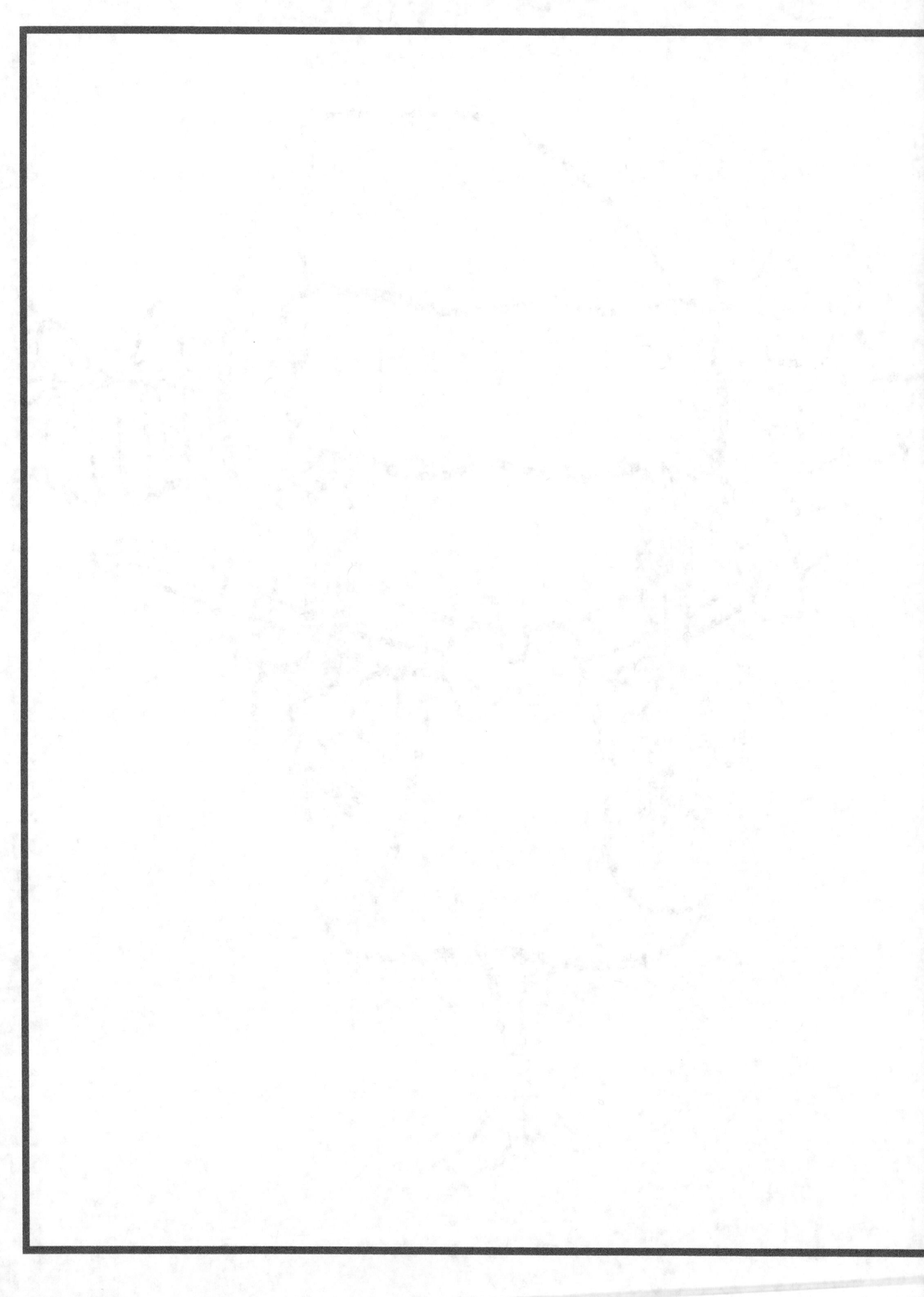

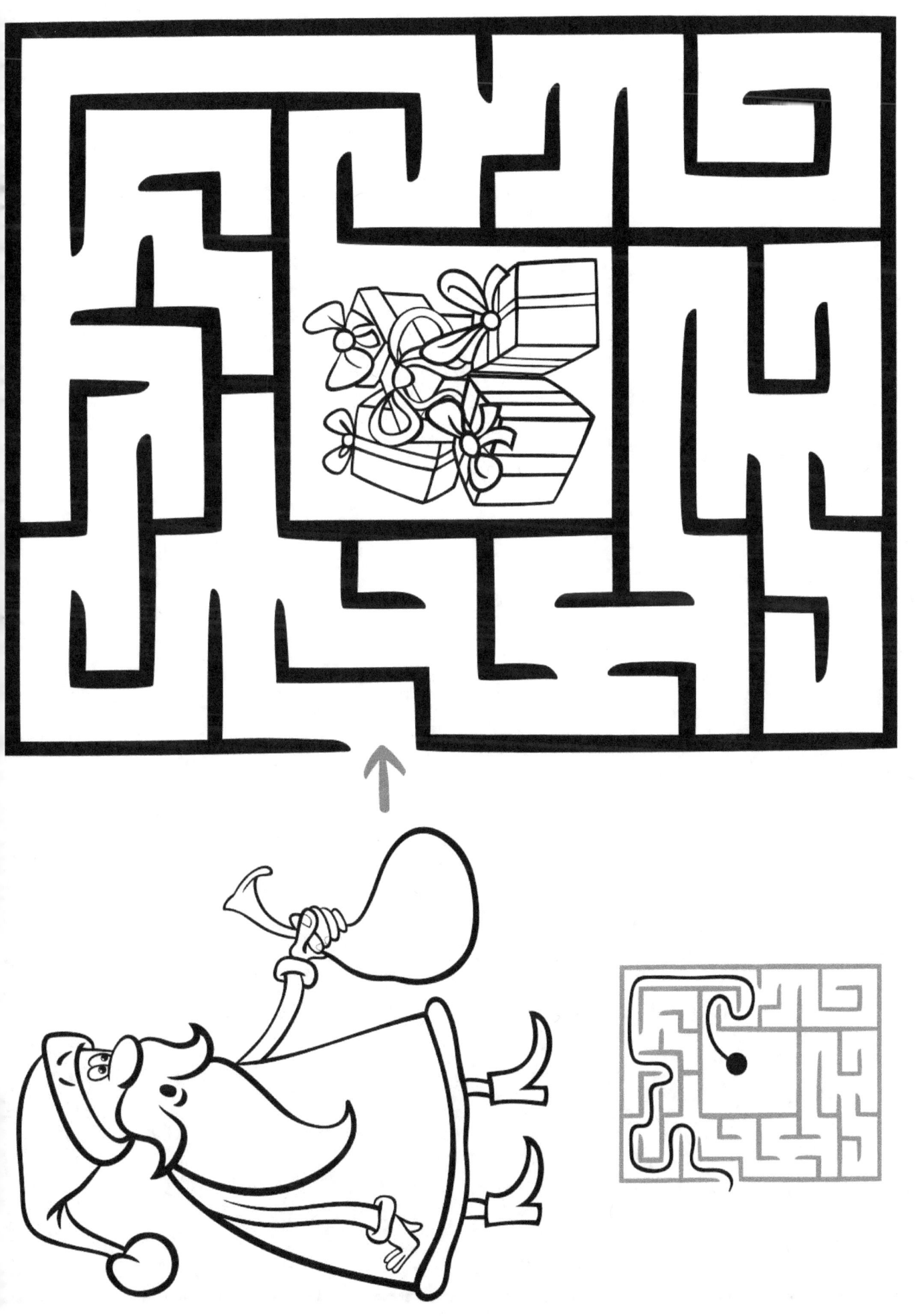

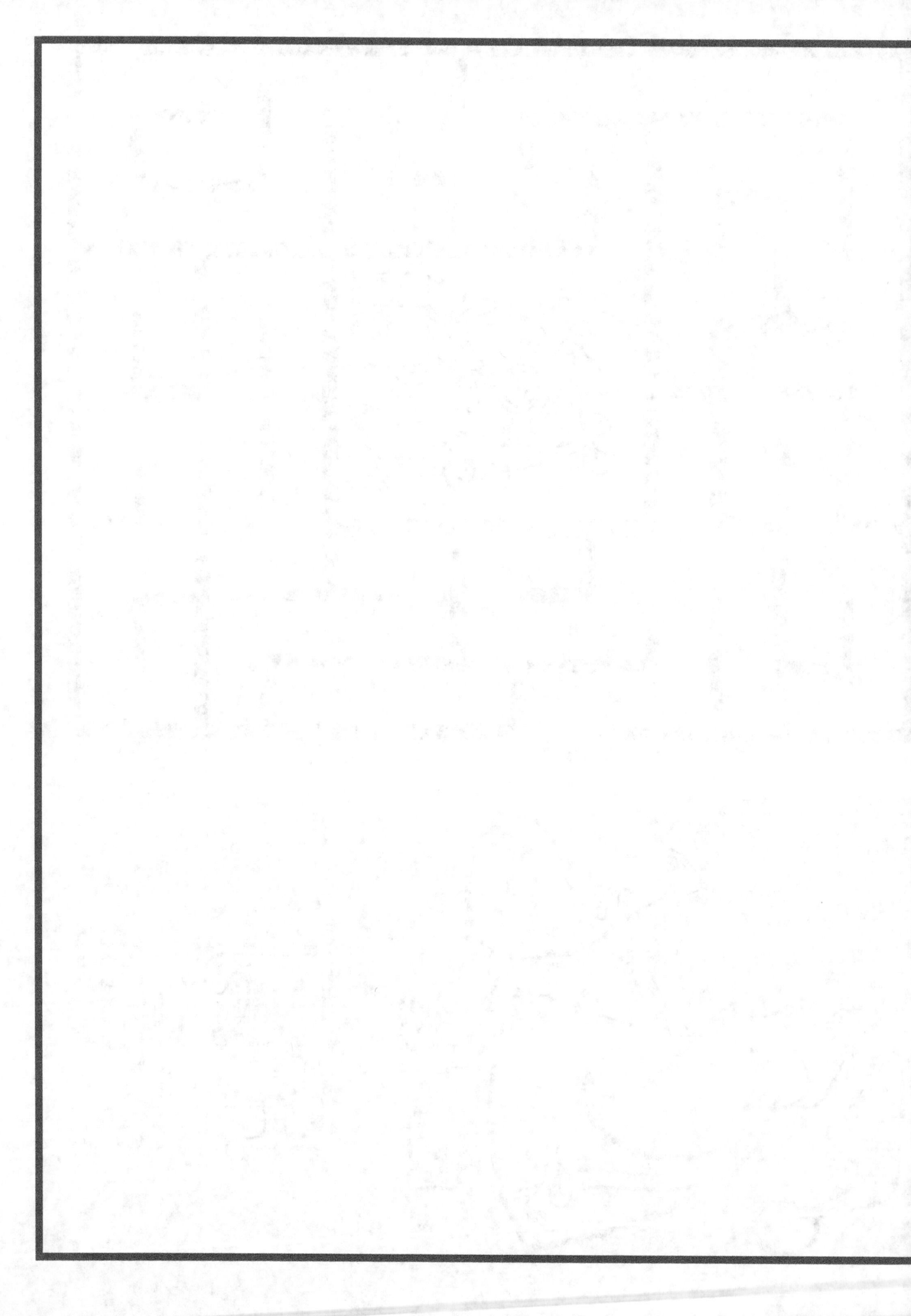

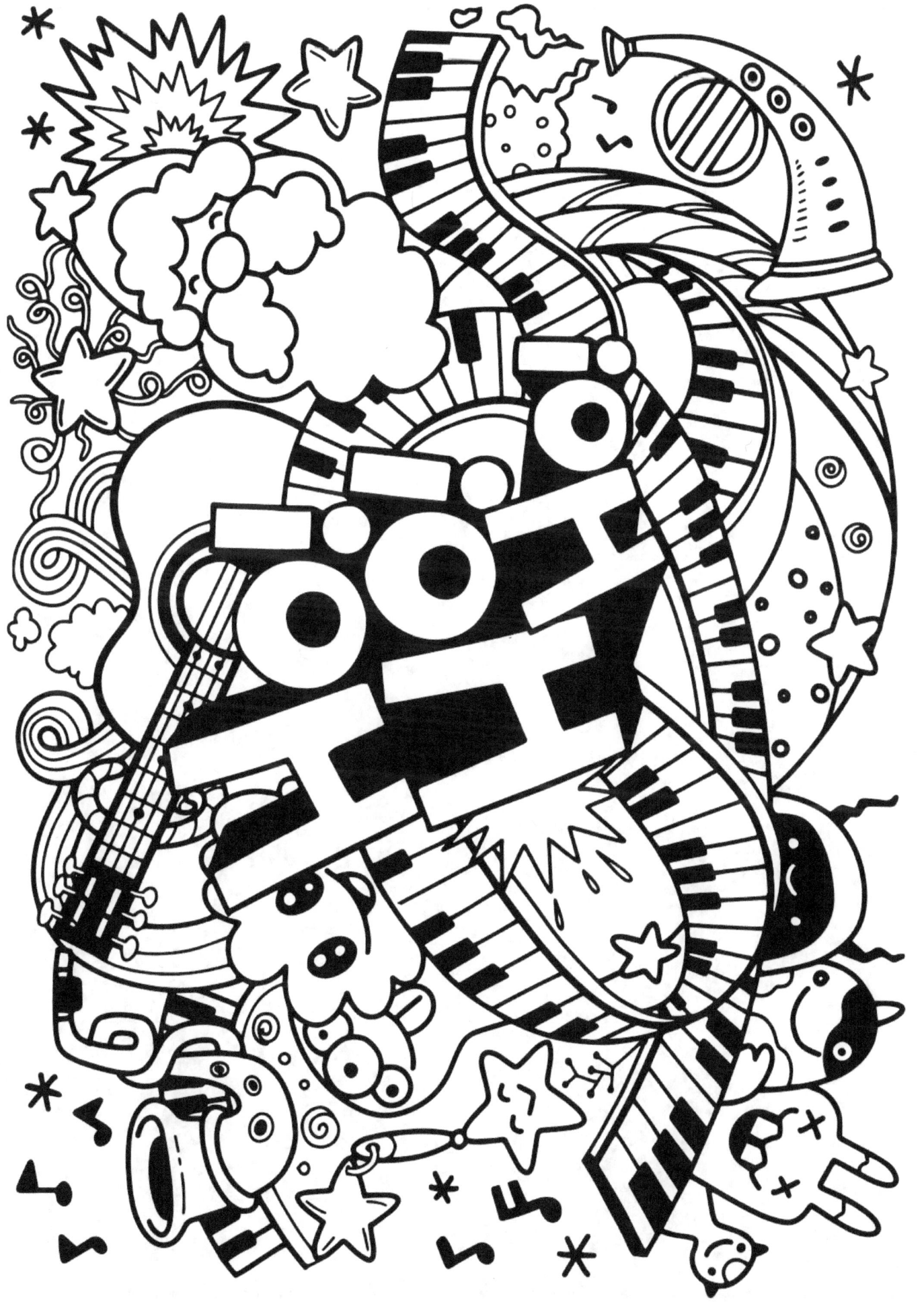

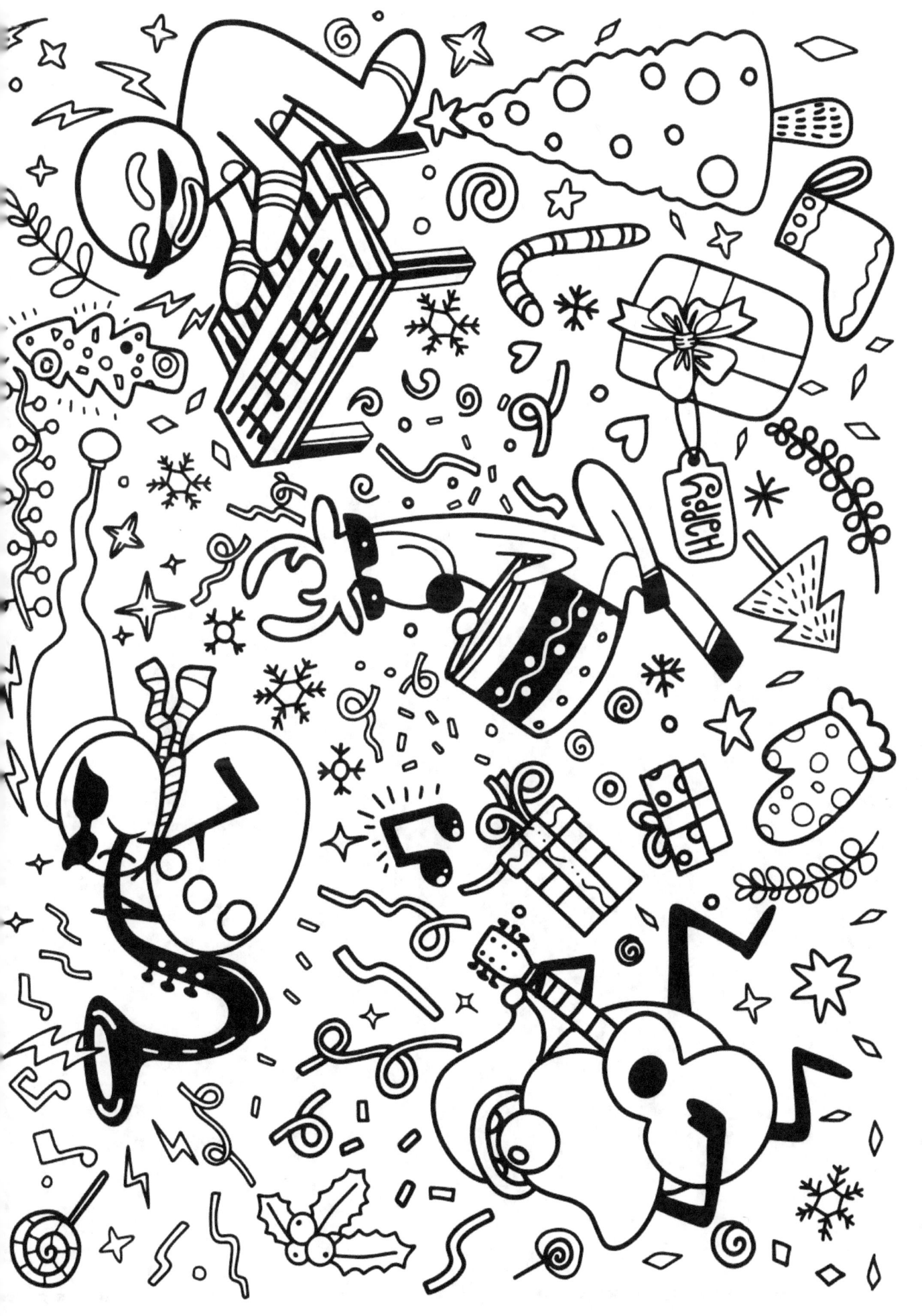

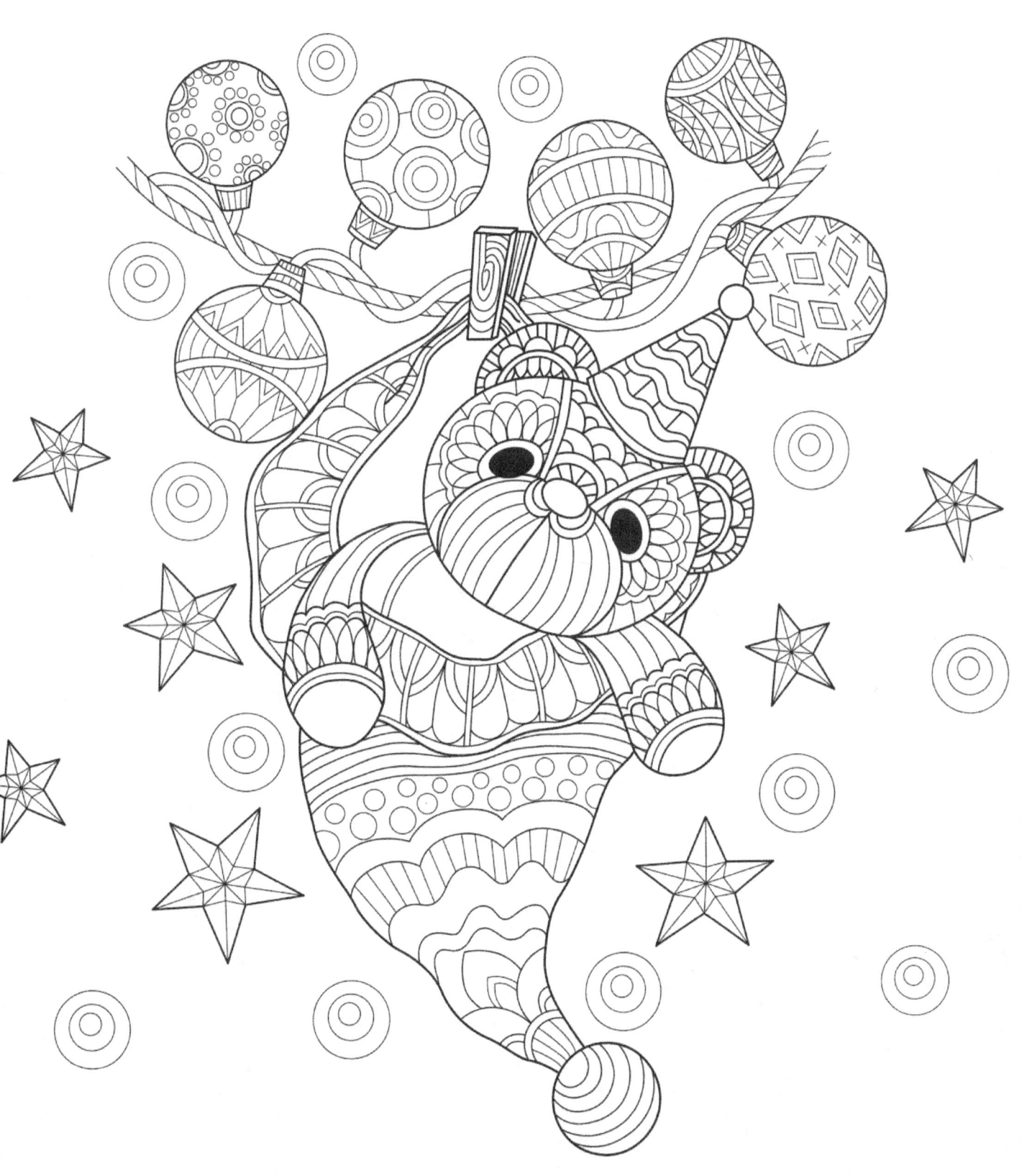

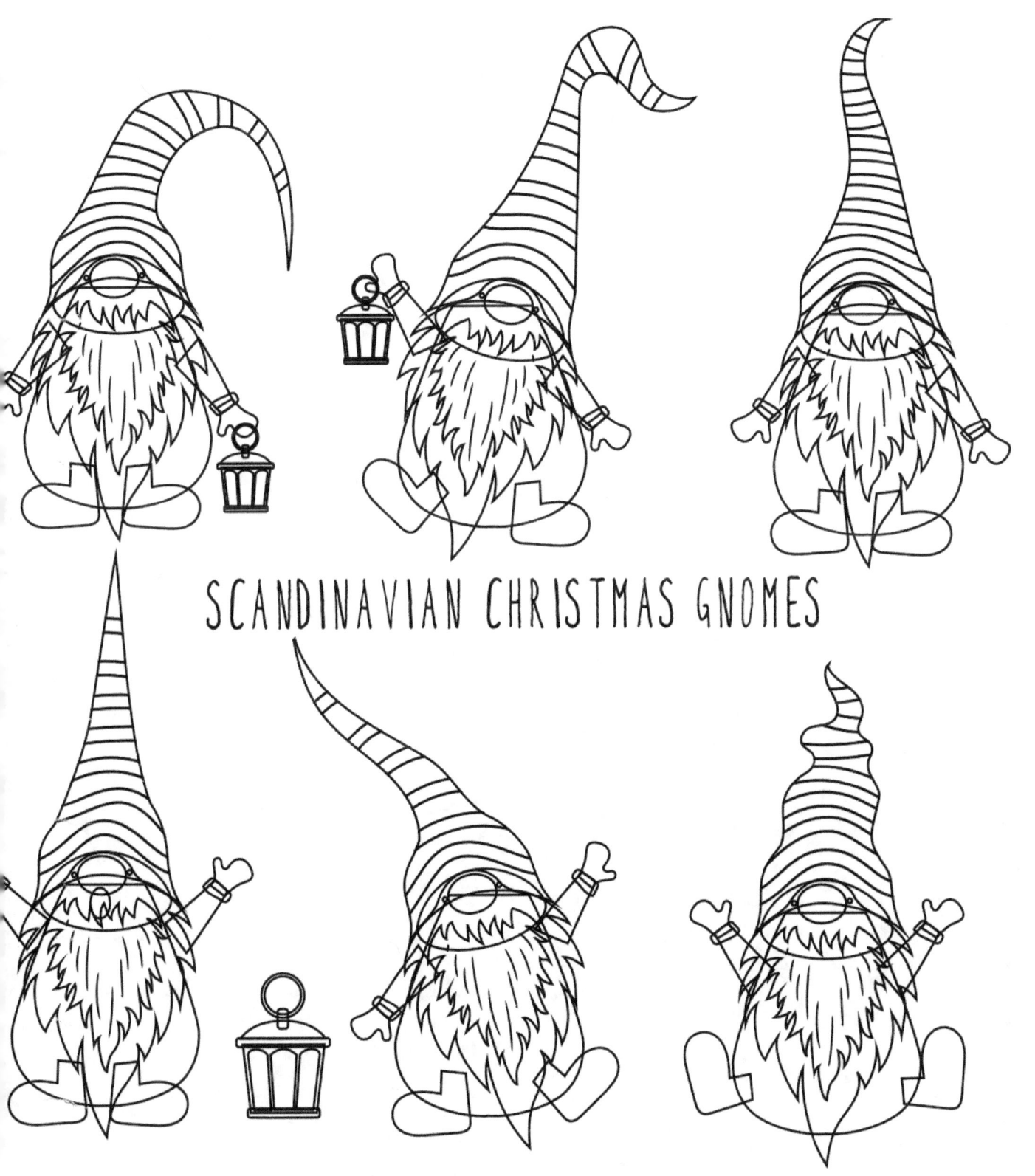

SCANDINAVIAN CHRISTMAS GNOMES

www.ingramcontent.com/pod-product-compliance
Lightning Source LLC
Chambersburg PA
CBHW082154230526
45467CB00044B/3310